STEVE O RENO'S

# FANTASY BOUND

## THE ART OF IMAGINATIVE DISTRESS

**VOLUME ONE**

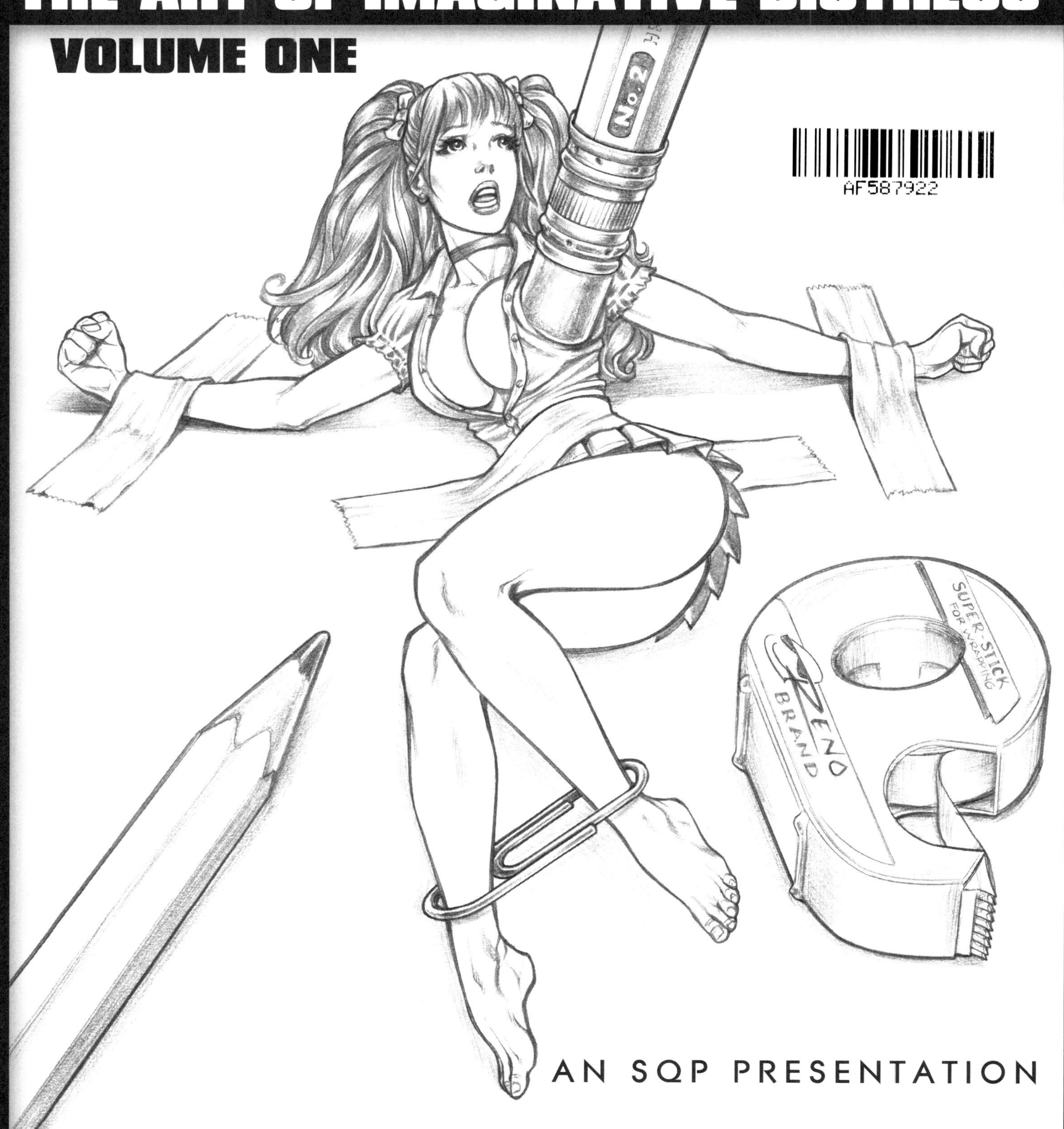


AN SQP PRESENTATION

# Everybody Needs a Fantasy Fetish

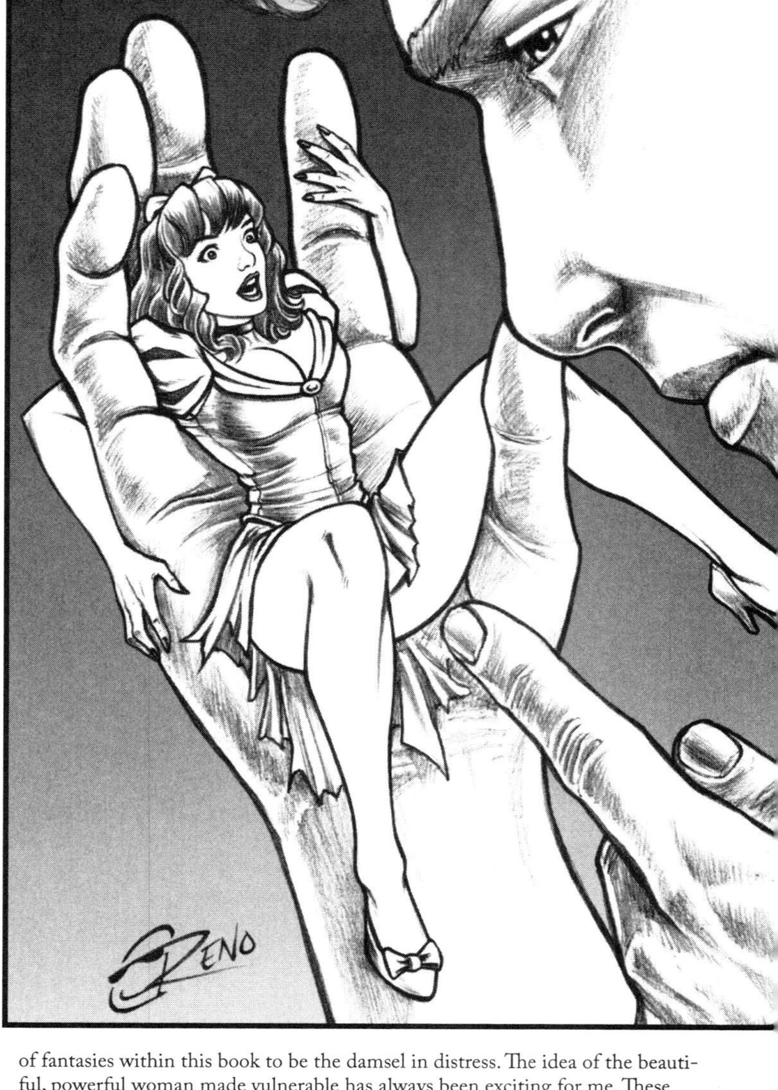


I've always thought it was funny how almost any fetish can be thought of as perverse by someone else. I guess it's part of our nature to see anything that doesn't turn us on personally as being something weird if another person is aroused by it. I have to admit, I've been just as guilty in thinking it, but several years ago I started delving into several different fantasies that various people were sharing with me. My entire life, I was always fascinated by idea of the 'Damsel in Distress'. In TV shows, movies, comics, whatever the genre, if the beautiful heroine was captured by some dastardly villain, I was hooked!

As I got older, I started discovering new ways that the damsels could be caught and put in their delicious distresses. Sometimes it might be tentacles, sometimes it might be giants and shrunken women, sometimes it was crazy machines that held them in their mechanical clutches. As the age of the internet allowed me to post my drawings where anyone around the world could see them, I was often contacted by people asking if I had ever thought of drawing [Insert Character Here] in [Insert Peril Here]. Well, anytime something new to me came up, rather than discounting the idea of that fetish, I'd try and wrap my head around it and see what it was that they found sexy about it. It was always an extremely eye opening experience.

I've always thought that regular sex (what I like to call 'Discovery Channel Sex') was for the physical body, and that a fetish was sex for the mind. Over time, I've come to see that it can be one of the most powerful aspects of human sexuality. Talking to people about their particular fetishes over the years, I've found that most discovered them at a very early age. There was always something they saw in their youth that deeply intrigued them for some inexplicable reason. From hearing so many similar stories, I still don't know if it was something ingrained in them, or if it was the first impact they felt during their sexual awakening that just stuck with them.

Whatever the case, I think for a person to NOT have a fetish, to never indulge in the idea of mental sexual stimulation, they are missing out on one of life's greatest pleasures. So what is a FANTASY fetish as opposed to a typical fetish? I think of a typical fetish as being something like an infatuation with a particular body part or perhaps an item of clothing. It might be enjoying an act of pleasure that stimulates you but is not necessarily part of the act of sex. I see TYPICAL as sexualizing the tangible.

A FANTASY fetish, on the other hand, is something beyond the realm of reality or something you couldn't experience in your normal, everyday life. One couldn't simply shoot an array of tentacles from their crotch and wrap up a group of buxom anime schoolgirls. One could not simply BE a giant, or be grabbed and sexually played with by one. In your life, you will never be an alien creature holding a sexy squadron of space babes in futuristic bondage, or a demonic hellspawn that has captured a fallen angel, or a super genius villain who places heroines in all kinds of devious devices .... but through fantasy, you can be ALL these things.

We might read superhero comic books or fantasy novels, see blockbuster action movies or watch clever sci-fi tv shows, knowing none of these things could ever happen in real life. But we nevertheless enjoy losing ourselves in these larger than life, epic fantasies, eagerly awaiting each new experience they bring us. So what I've always locked for was that same level of over the top fun mixed with a sexually charged twist. You'll find the underlying element to the wide variety of fantasies within this book to be the damsel in distress. The idea of the beautiful, powerful woman made vulnerable has always been exciting for me. These pictures are all things that, for the most part, I could never experience in real life. Each frame is a moment that has a before and after to play around with in your mind. To wonder how the girls got into their predicaments, then to imagine what will happen to them next and how they will ultimately get free. I've always believed that a vivid imagination can create fantasies that feel as real as memories, and just like those comics, novels, movies, and tv shows ...the experience is all in the mind.


Steve O. Reno
Master of the Damsel
Supreme Leader of the Renogades
www.steveoreno.deviantart.com
renoart@hotmail.com


**Steve O Reno's Fantasy Bound**
**The Art of Imaginative Distress**
**Volume 1**



Book design by Grassy Knoll Studios.
Published by
SQP Inc.
PO Box 248 - Columbus, NJ 08022
Sal Quartuccio & Bob Keenan - Publishers


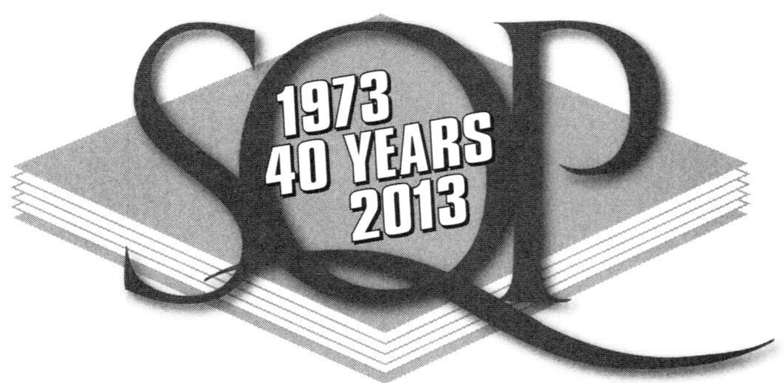

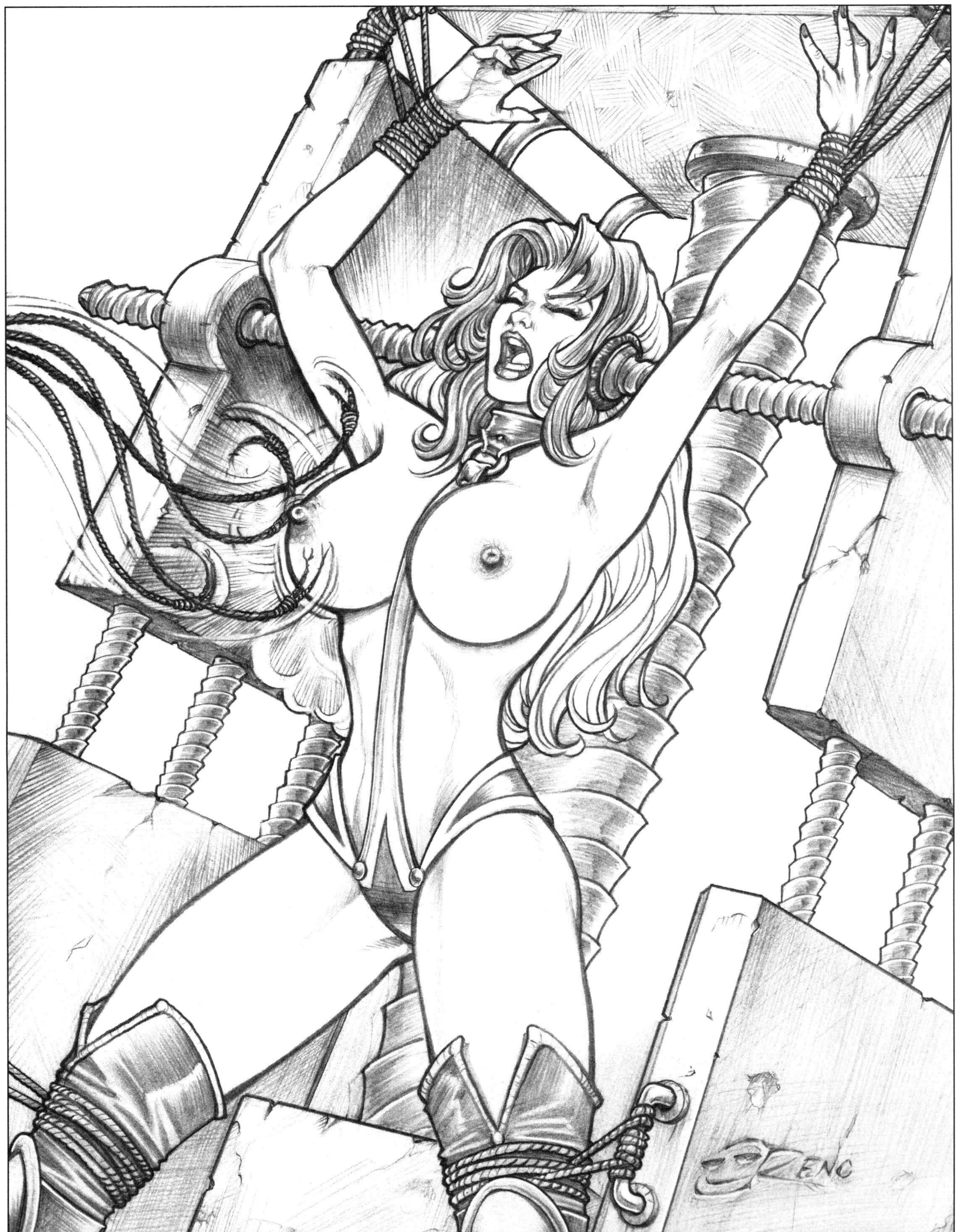

*Tarnished*

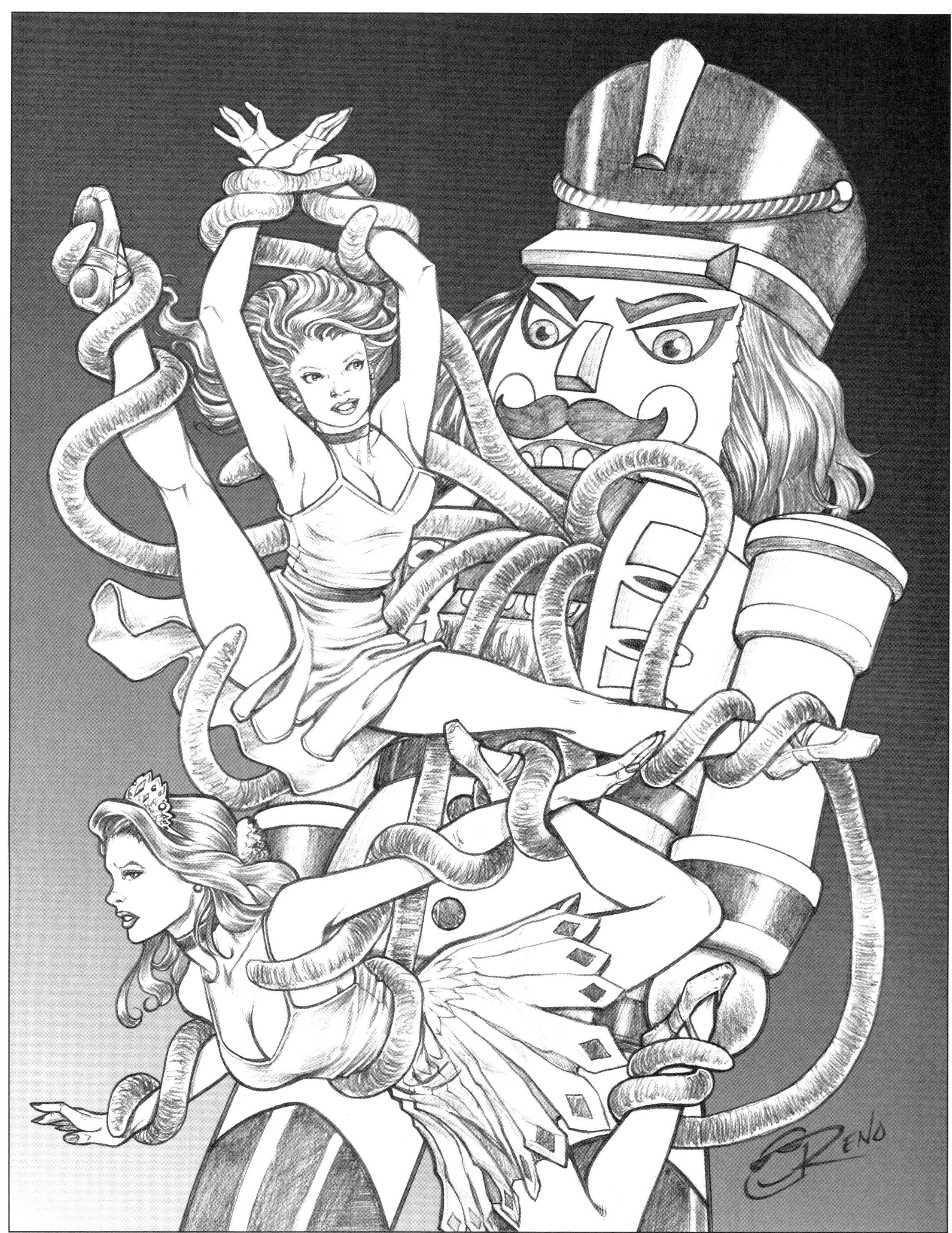

*Nut Kracken*

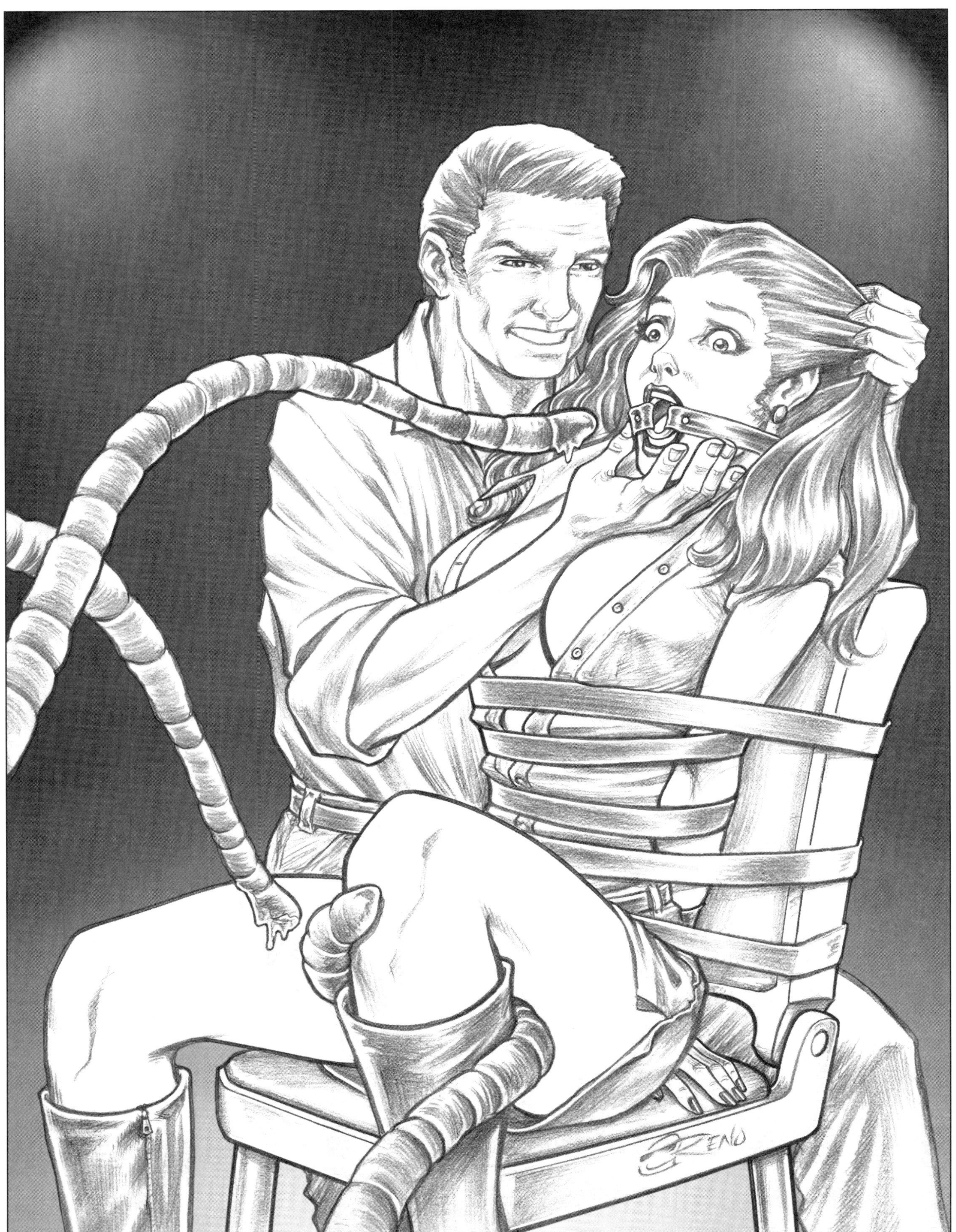

*Tentacle Chairs*

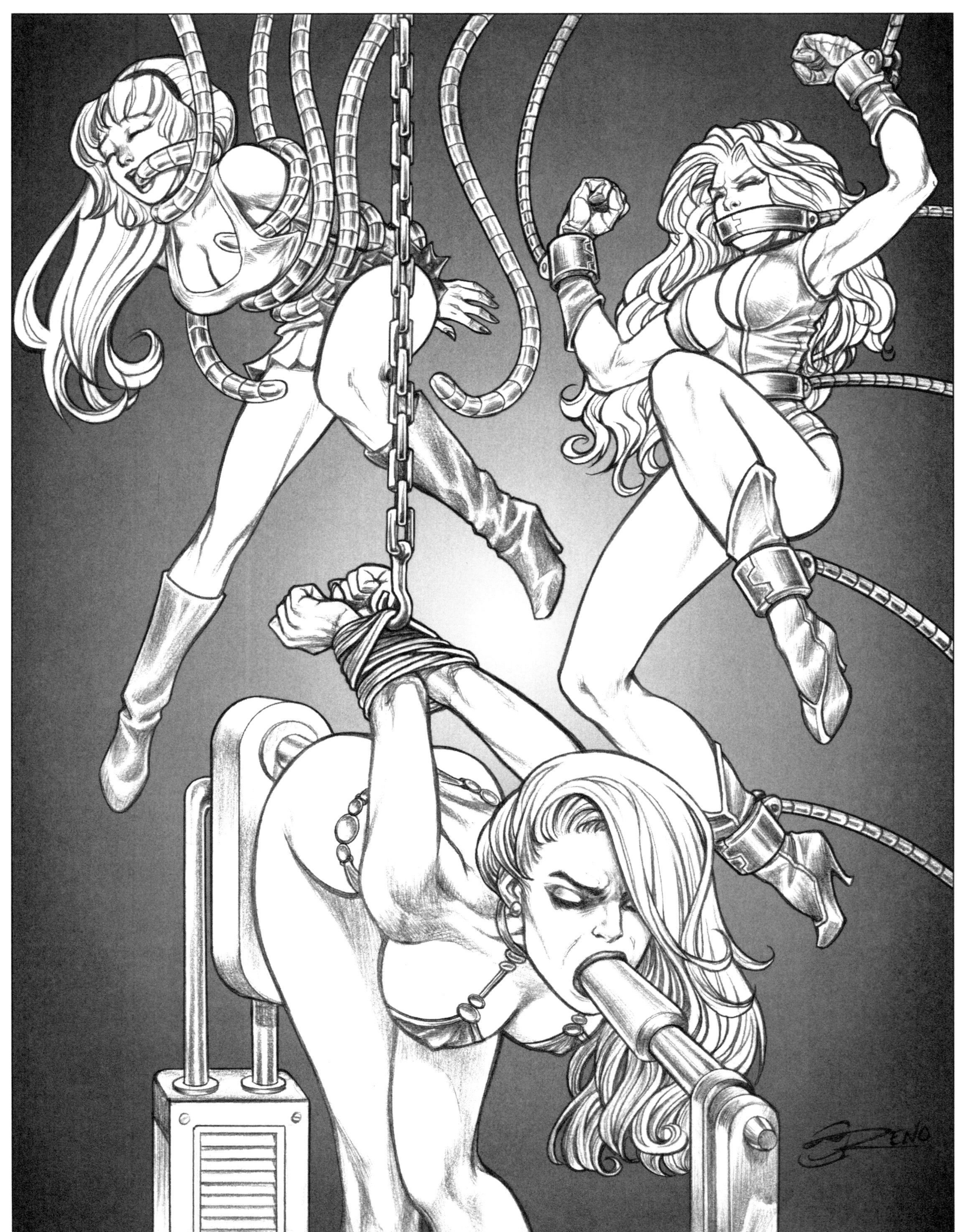

*Mechanical Problems*

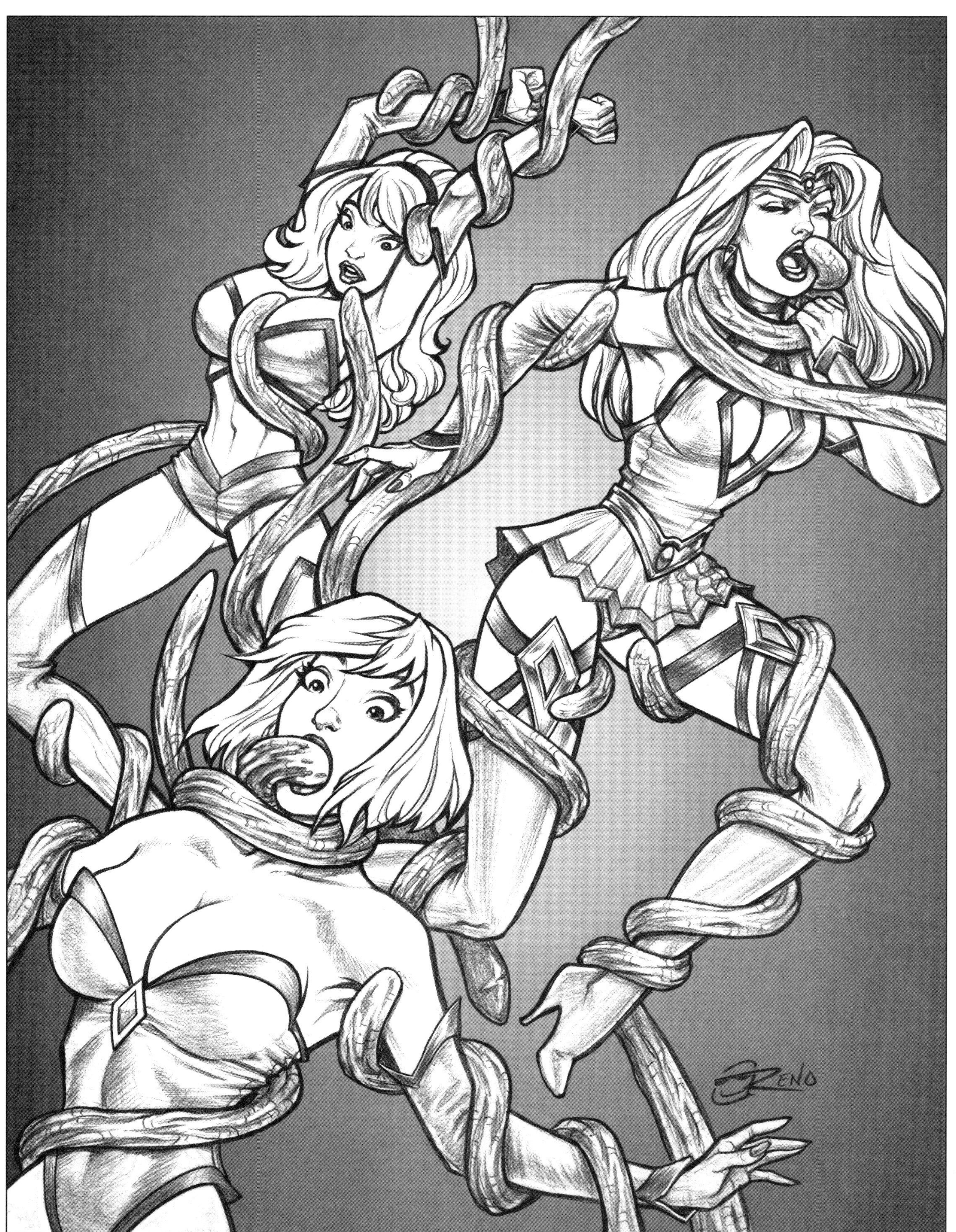

*Tentacle Difficulties*

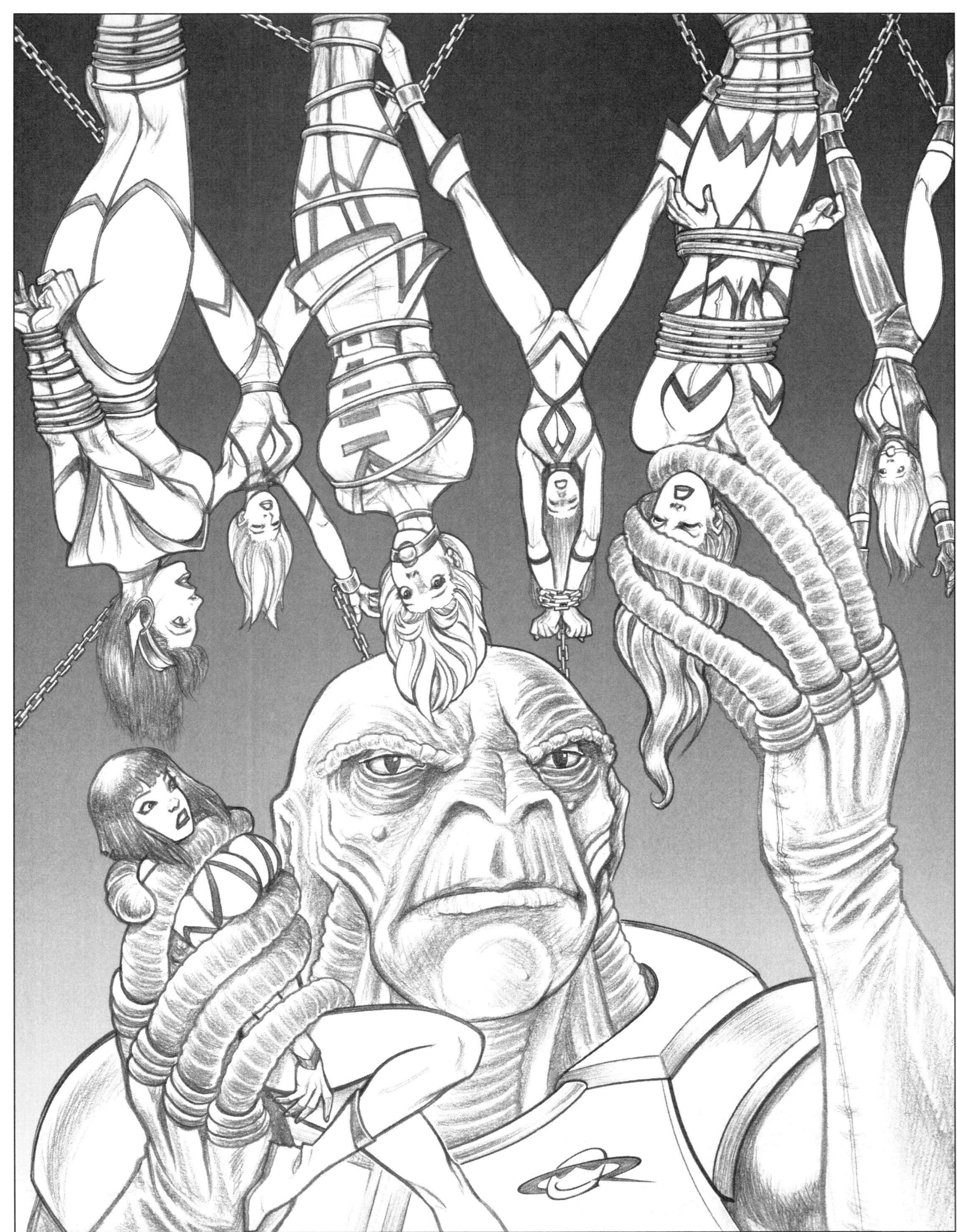

*Space Girl Squadron*

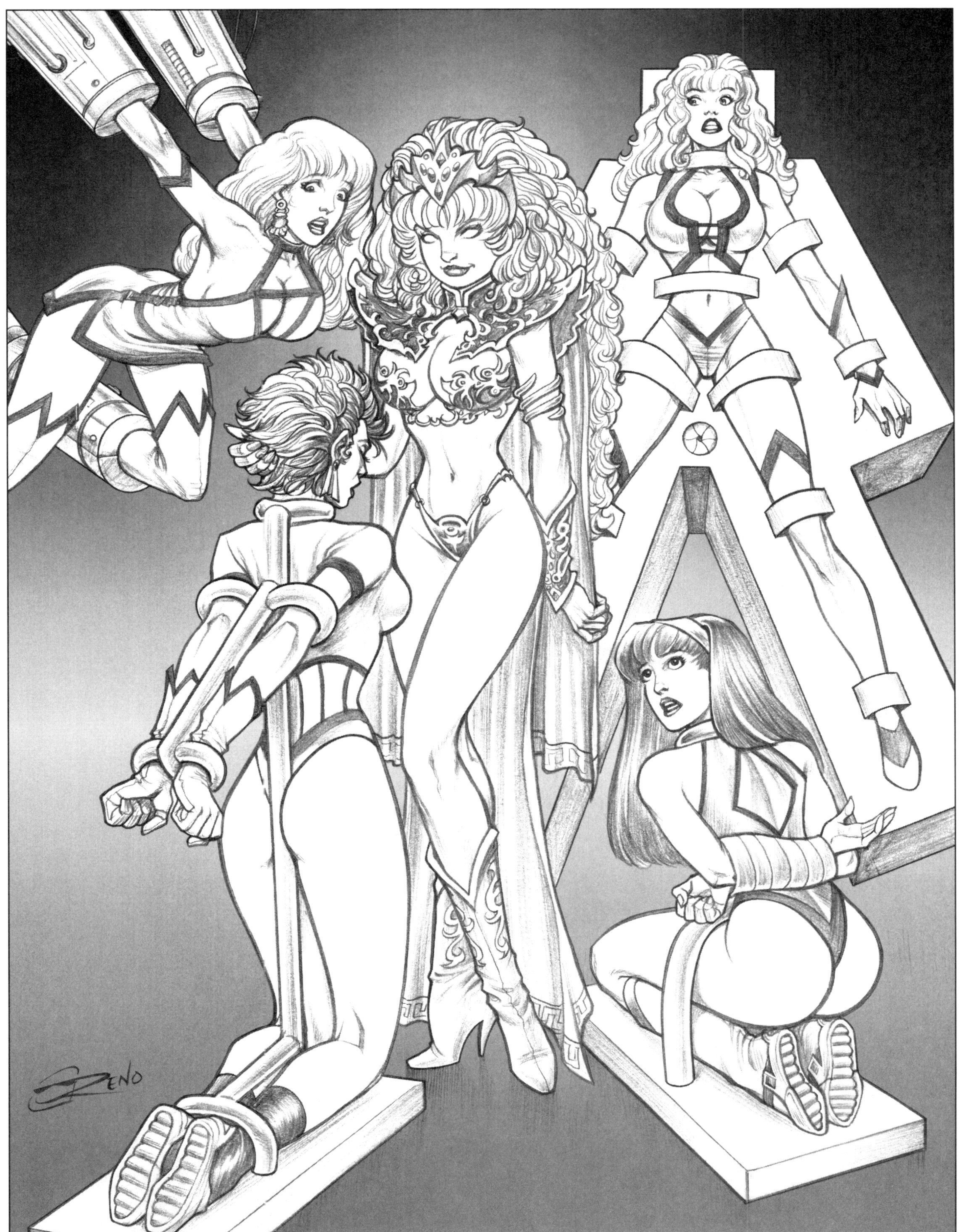

*Check Mate*

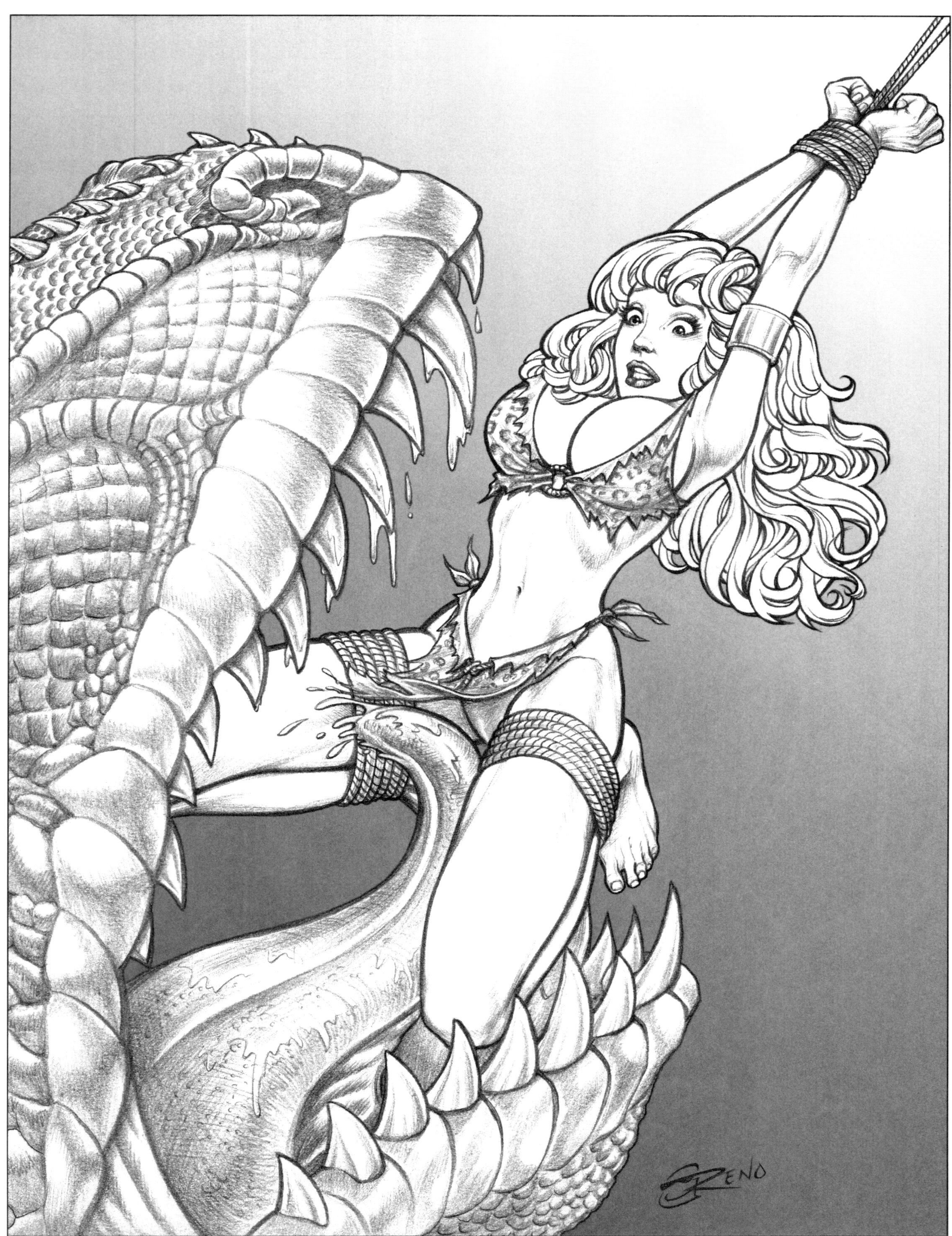


*Chomp*

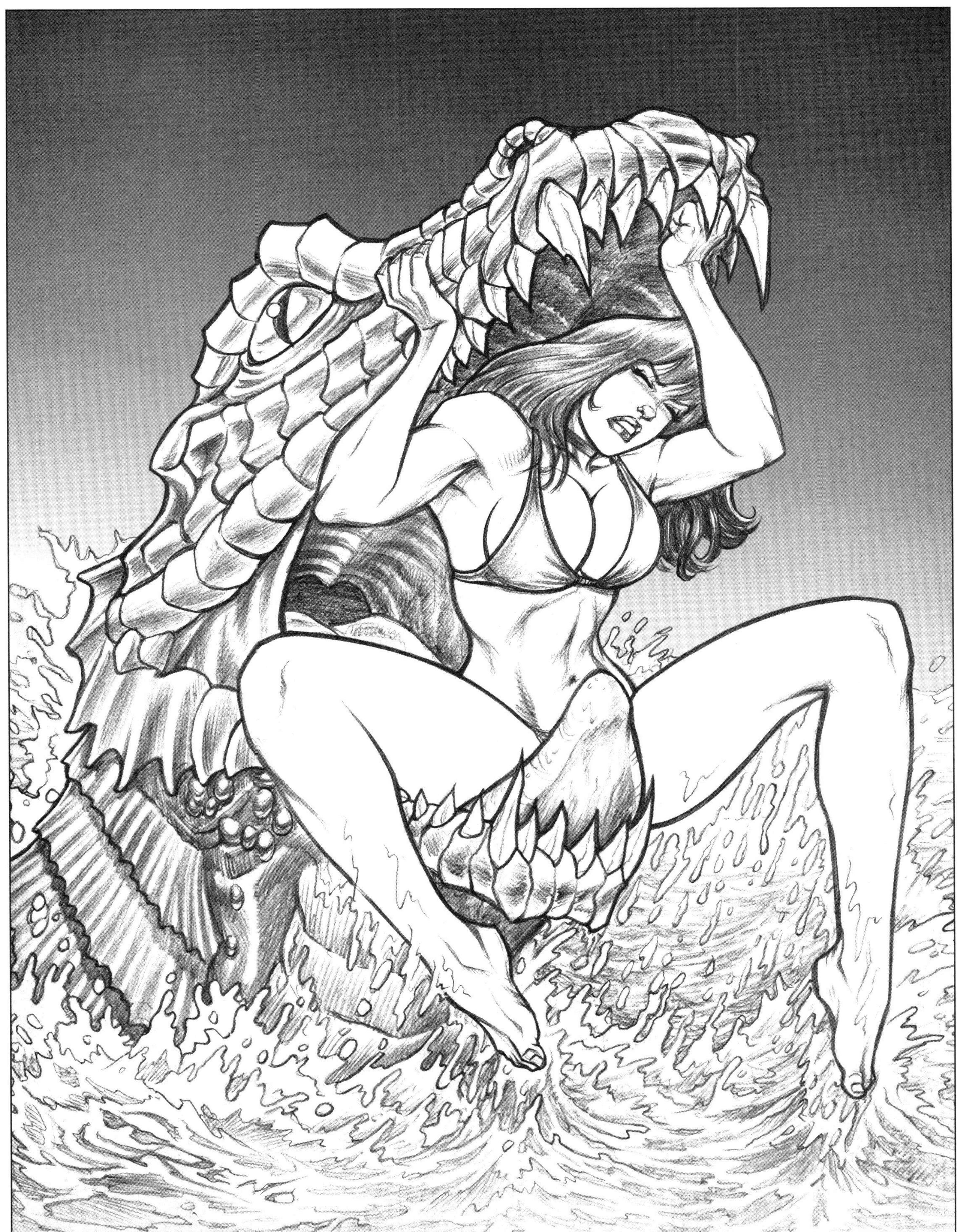

*Leviathan*

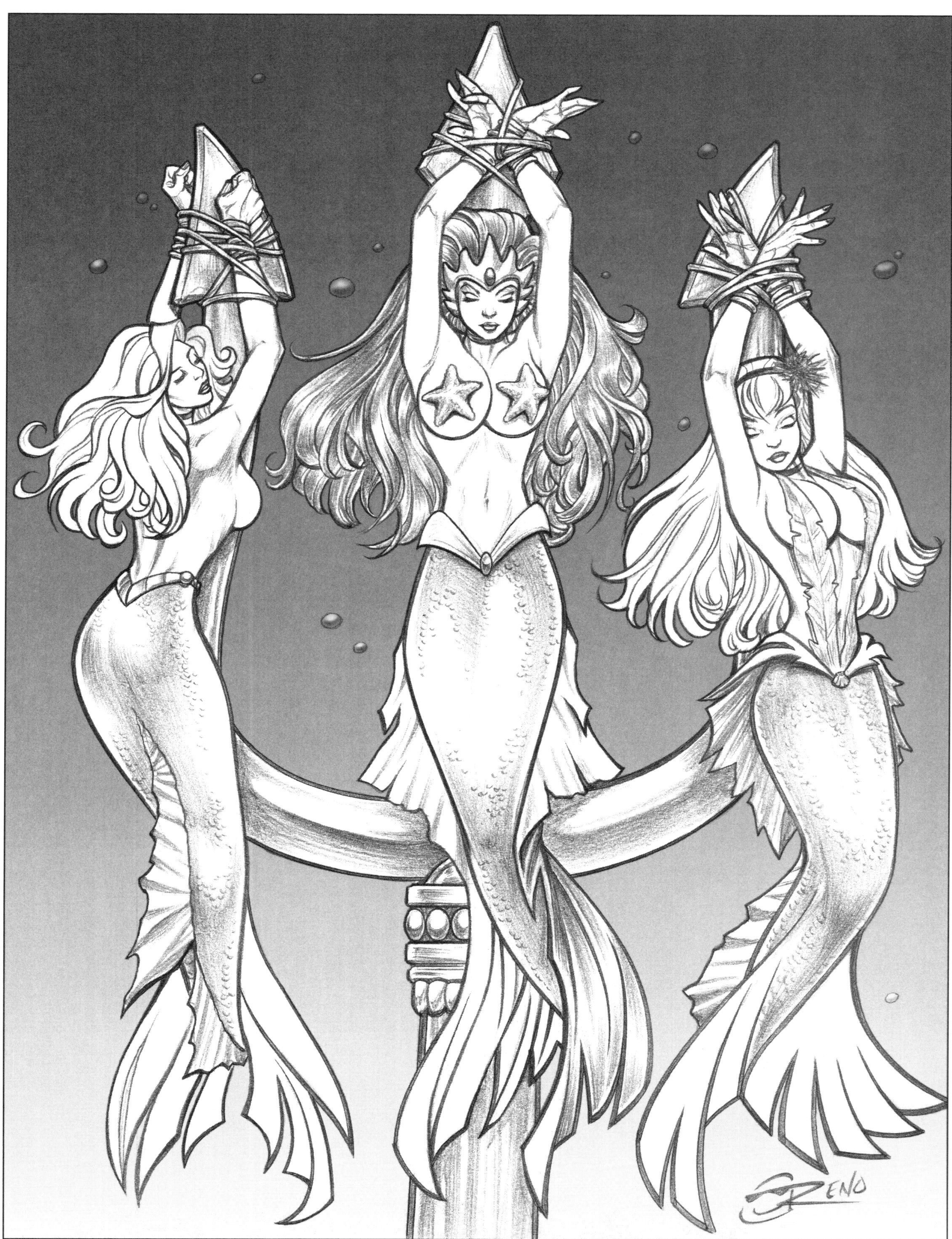


*Triton's Trident*

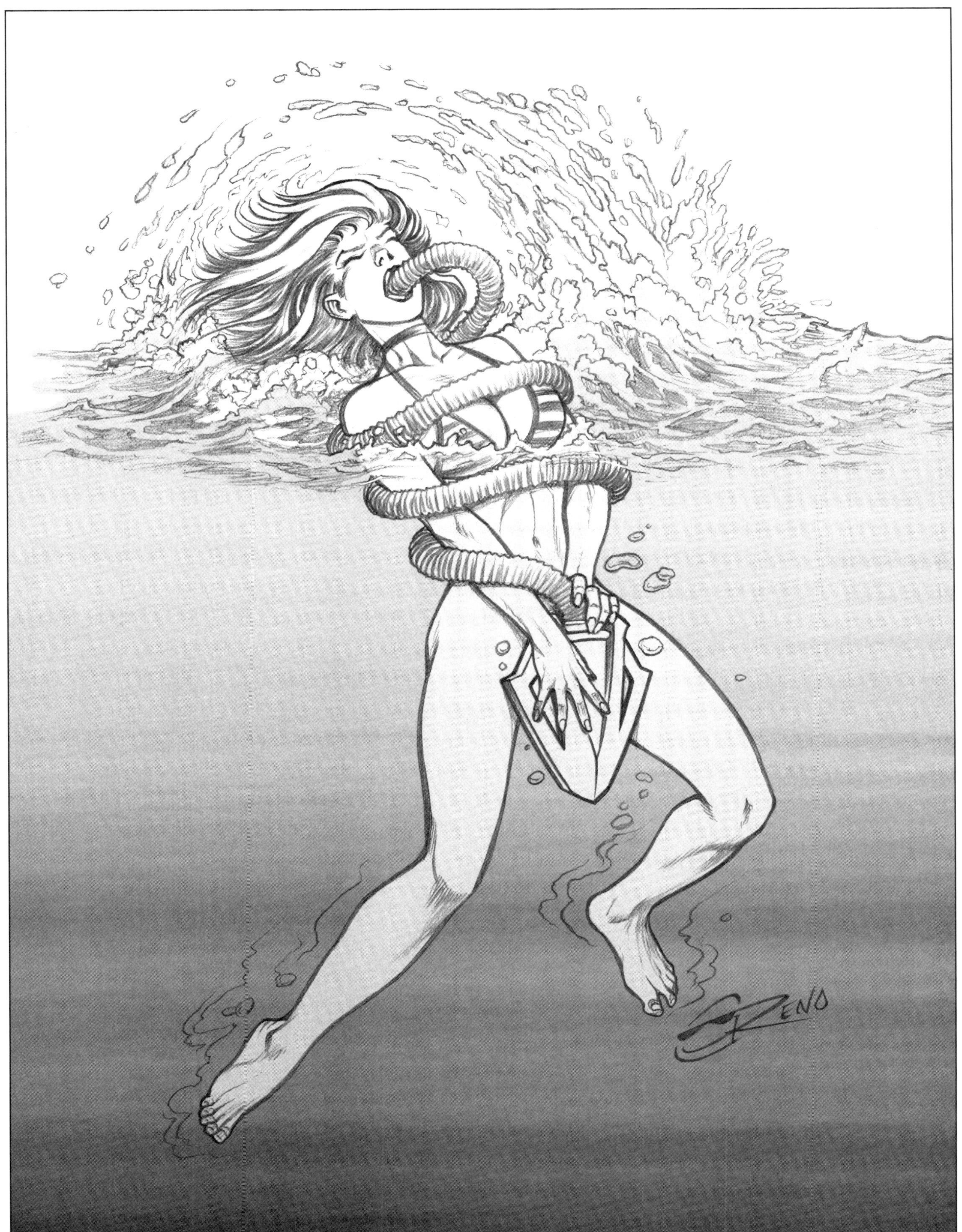

*Filter*

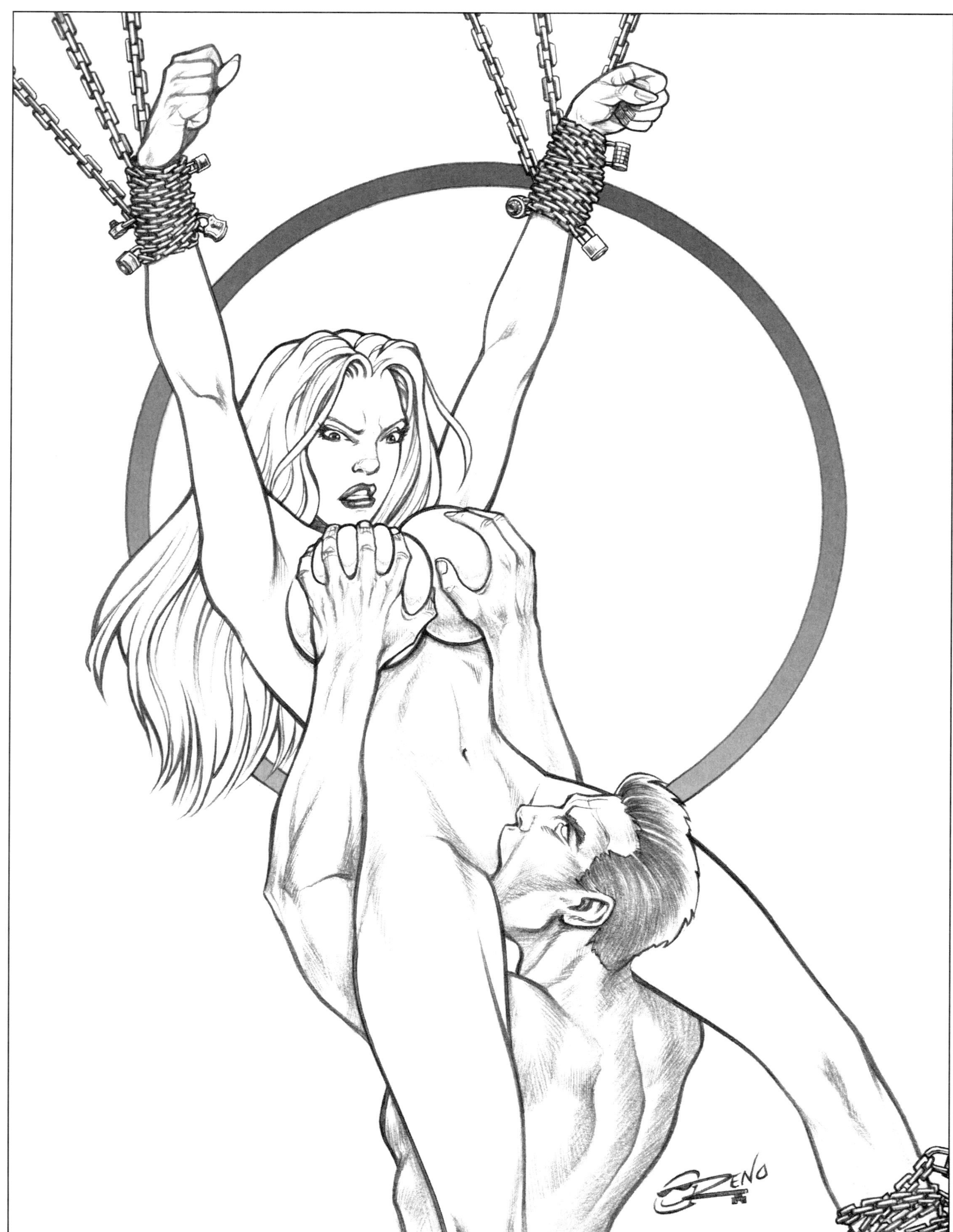

*Goldie Locks*

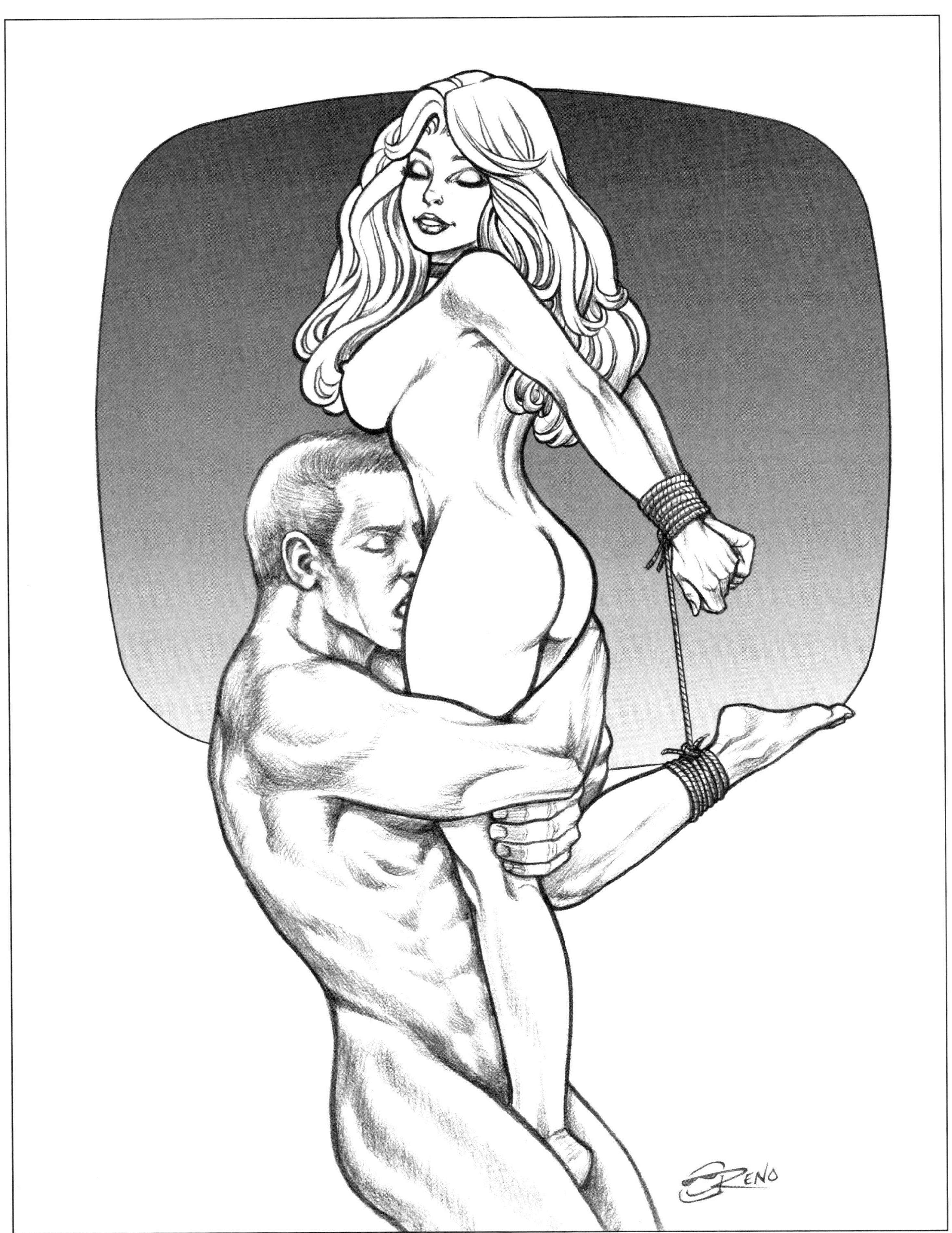


*Bare Necessities*

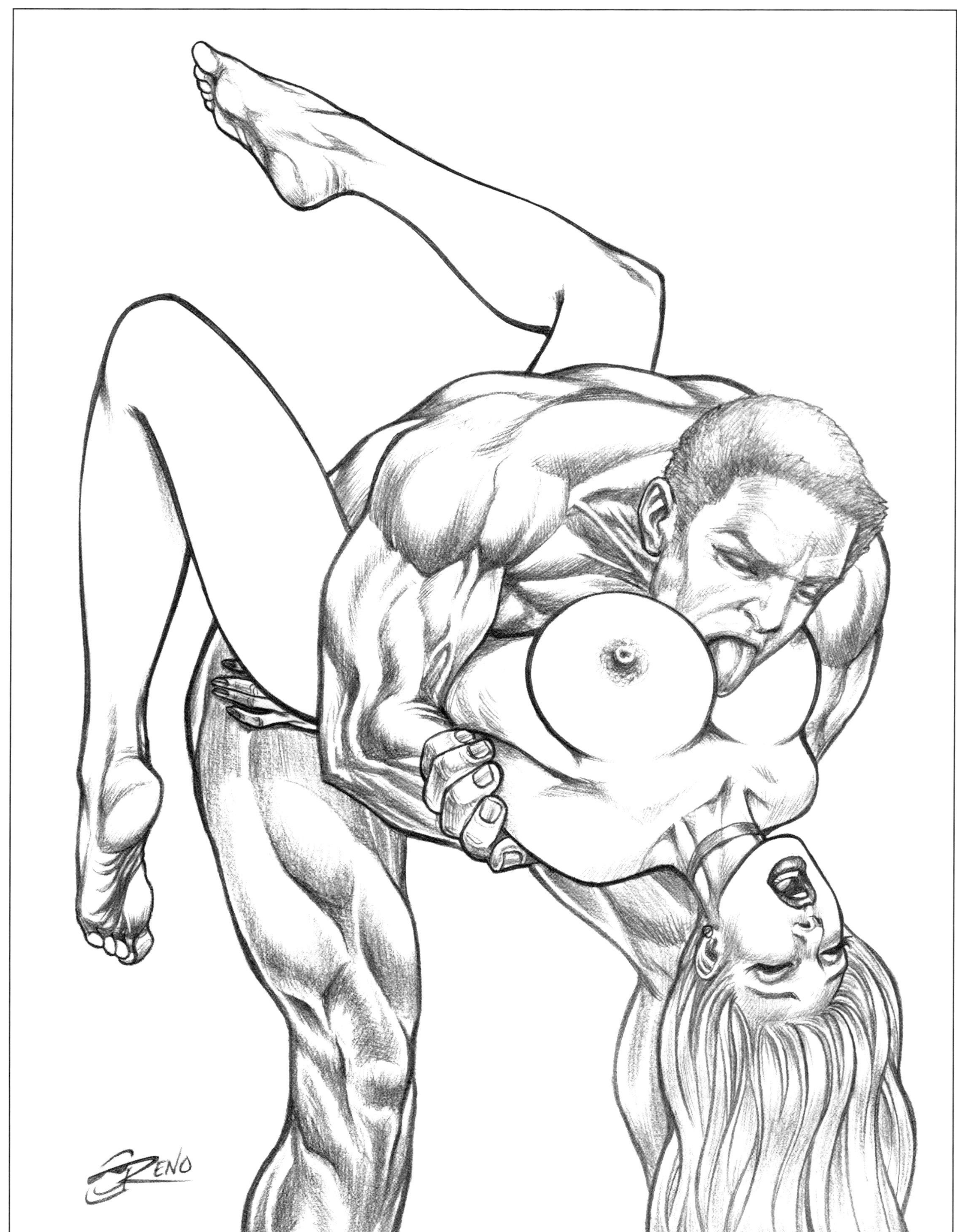

***Bare Hug***

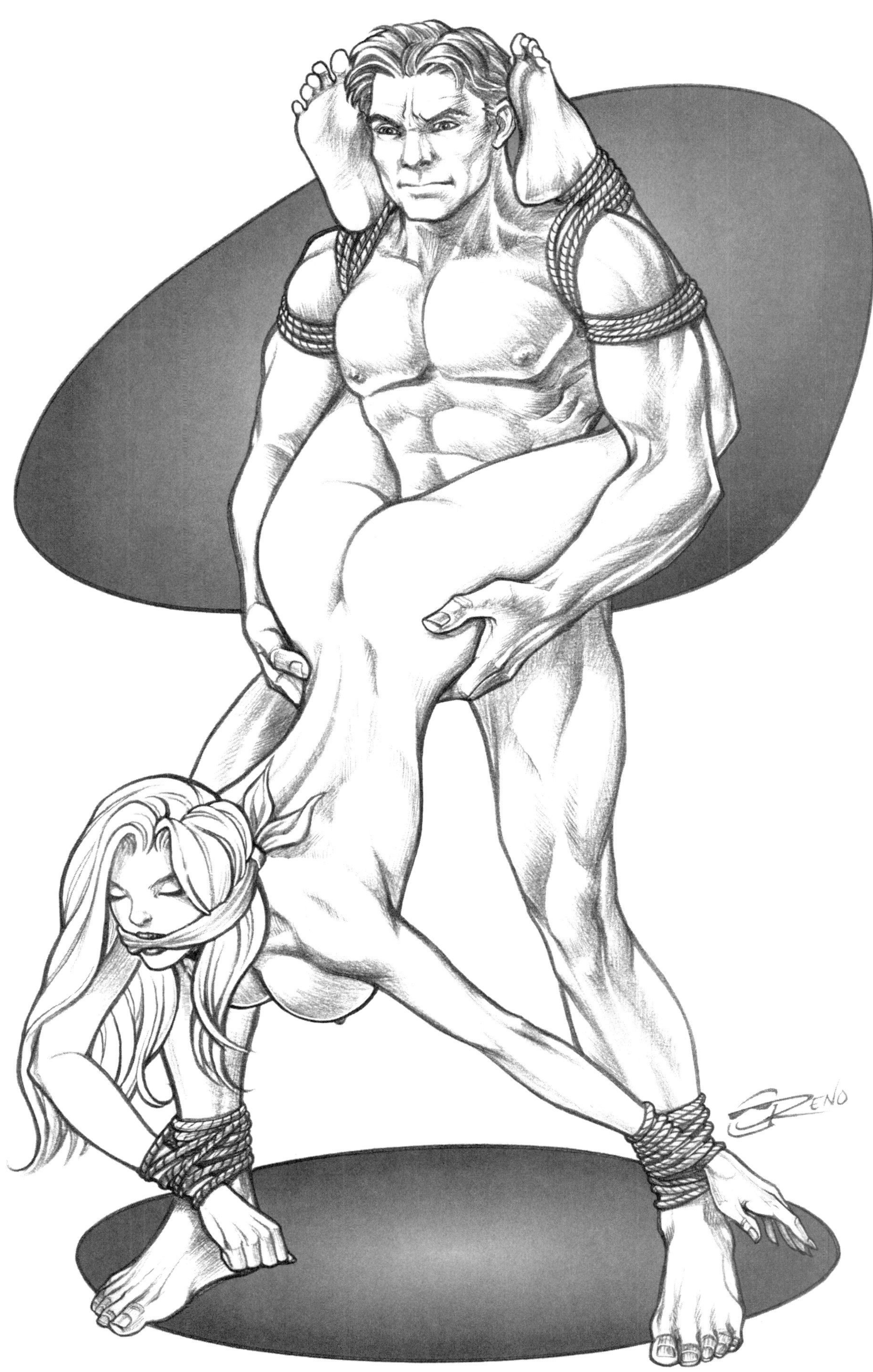

*Wheel Bare-O*

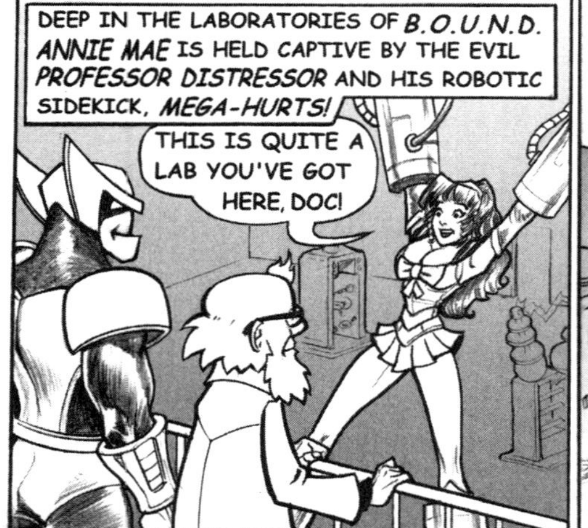
DEEP IN THE LABORATORIES OF B.O.U.N.D. ANNIE MAE IS HELD CAPTIVE BY THE EVIL PROFESSOR DISTRESSOR AND HIS ROBOTIC SIDEKICK, MEGA-HURTS!
THIS IS QUITE A LAB YOU'VE GOT HERE, DOC!

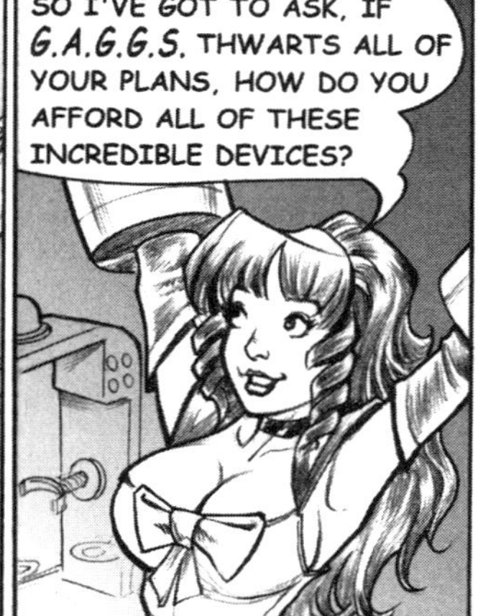
SO I'VE GOT TO ASK, IF G.A.G.G.S. THWARTS ALL OF YOUR PLANS, HOW DO YOU AFFORD ALL OF THESE INCREDIBLE DEVICES?

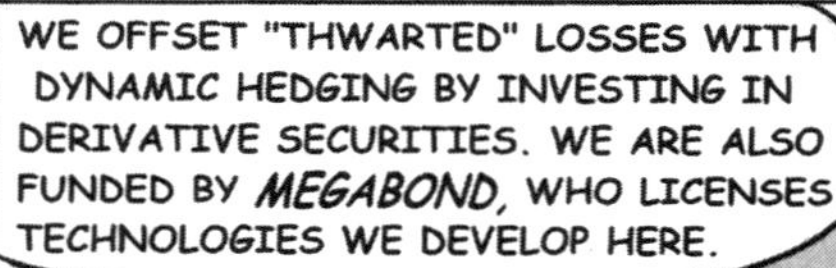
WE OFFSET "THWARTED" LOSSES WITH DYNAMIC HEDGING BY INVESTING IN DERIVATIVE SECURITIES. WE ARE ALSO FUNDED BY MEGABOND, WHO LICENSES TECHNOLOGIES WE DEVELOP HERE.

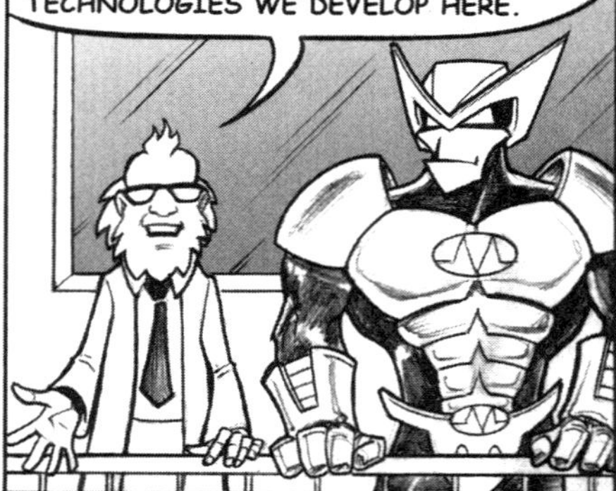

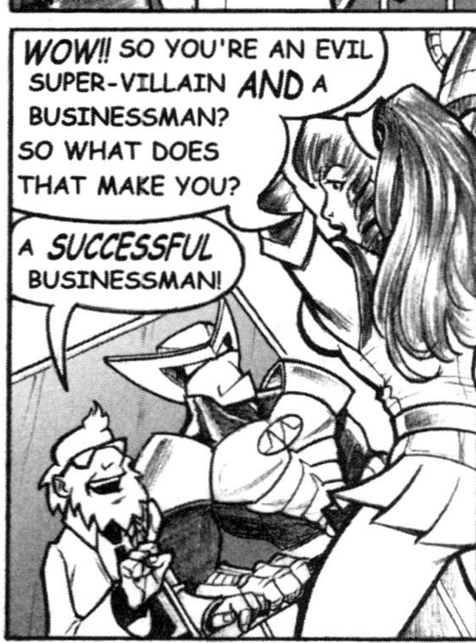
WOW!! SO YOU'RE AN EVIL SUPER-VILLAIN AND A BUSINESSMAN? SO WHAT DOES THAT MAKE YOU?
A SUCCESSFUL BUSINESSMAN!

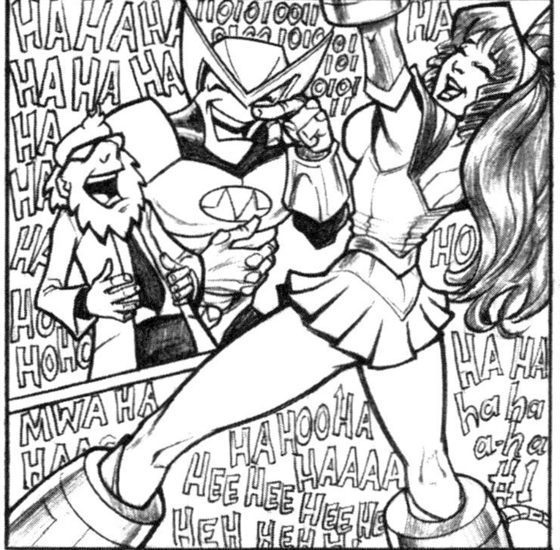
HA HA HA
MWA HA
HEE HEE
HEH HEH
ha ha a-ha

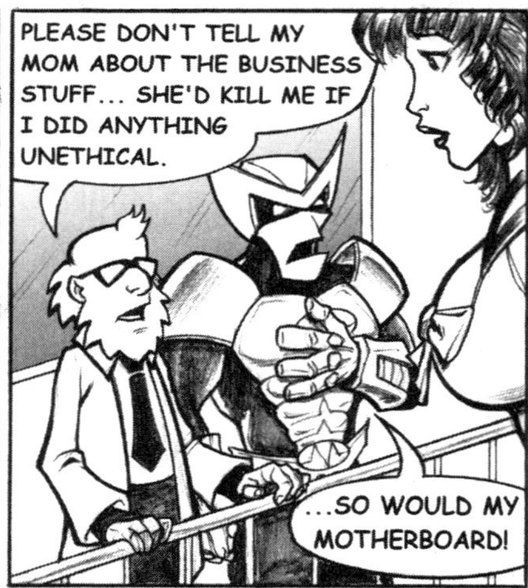
PLEASE DON'T TELL MY MOM ABOUT THE BUSINESS STUFF... SHE'D KILL ME IF I DID ANYTHING UNETHICAL.
...SO WOULD MY MOTHERBOARD!

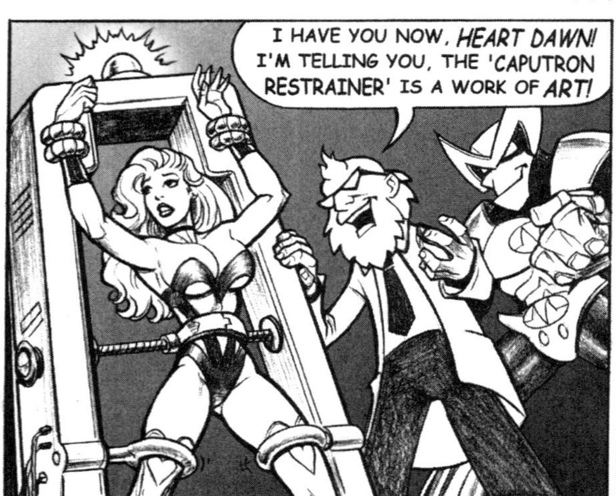
I HAVE YOU NOW, HEART DAWN! I'M TELLING YOU, THE 'CAPUTRON RESTRAINER' IS A WORK OF ART!

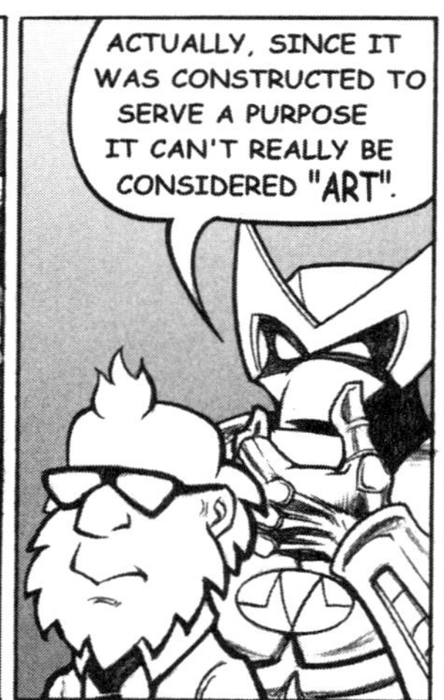
ACTUALLY, SINCE IT WAS CONSTRUCTED TO SERVE A PURPOSE IT CAN'T REALLY BE CONSIDERED "ART".

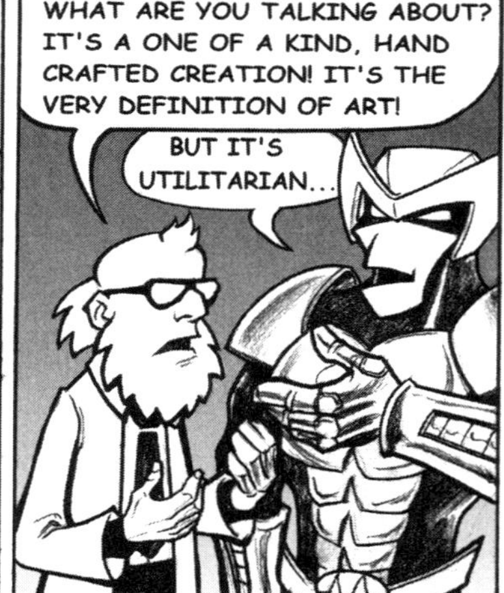
WHAT ARE YOU TALKING ABOUT? IT'S A ONE OF A KIND, HAND CRAFTED CREATION! IT'S THE VERY DEFINITION OF ART!
BUT IT'S UTILITARIAN...

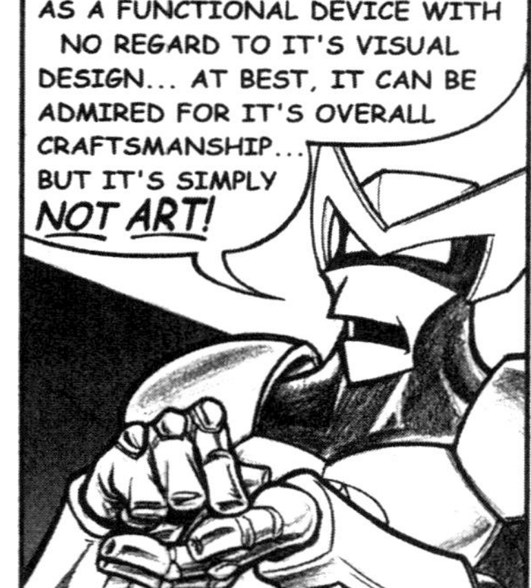
BUILT BY 'HENCHMAN FOR HIRE' AS A FUNCTIONAL DEVICE WITH NO REGARD TO IT'S VISUAL DESIGN... AT BEST, IT CAN BE ADMIRED FOR IT'S OVERALL CRAFTSMANSHIP... BUT IT'S SIMPLY NOT ART!

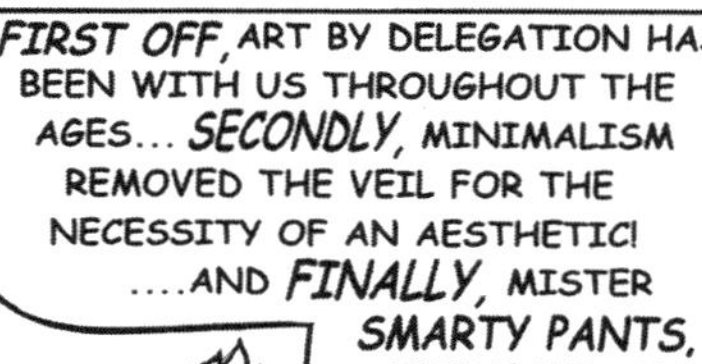
FIRST OFF, ART BY DELEGATION HAS BEEN WITH US THROUGHOUT THE AGES... SECONDLY, MINIMALISM REMOVED THE VEIL FOR THE NECESSITY OF AN AESTHETIC!

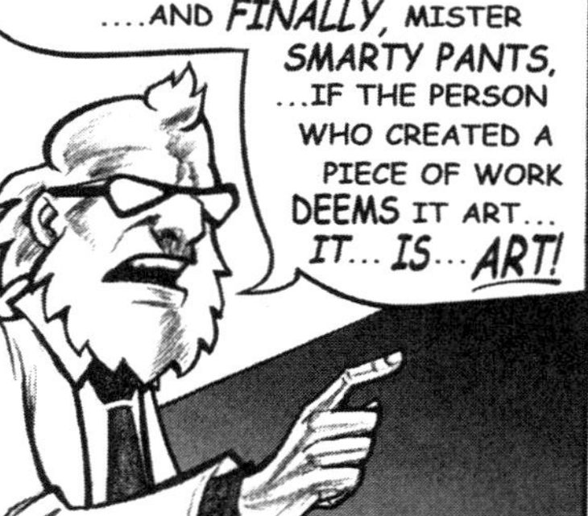
....AND FINALLY, MISTER SMARTY PANTS, ...IF THE PERSON WHO CREATED A PIECE OF WORK DEEMS IT ART... IT... IS... ART!

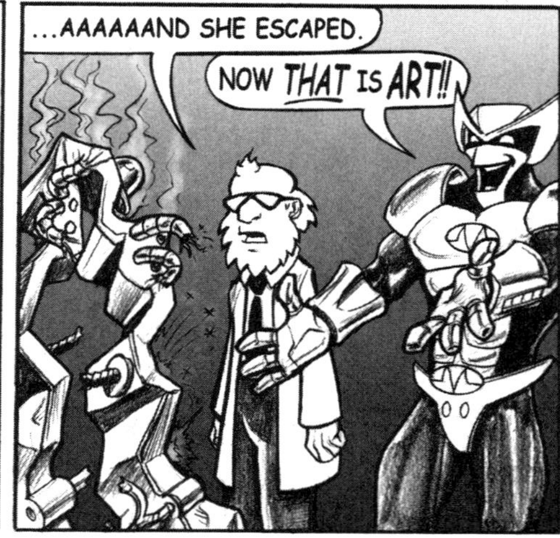
...AAAAAAND SHE ESCAPED.
NOW THAT IS ART!!

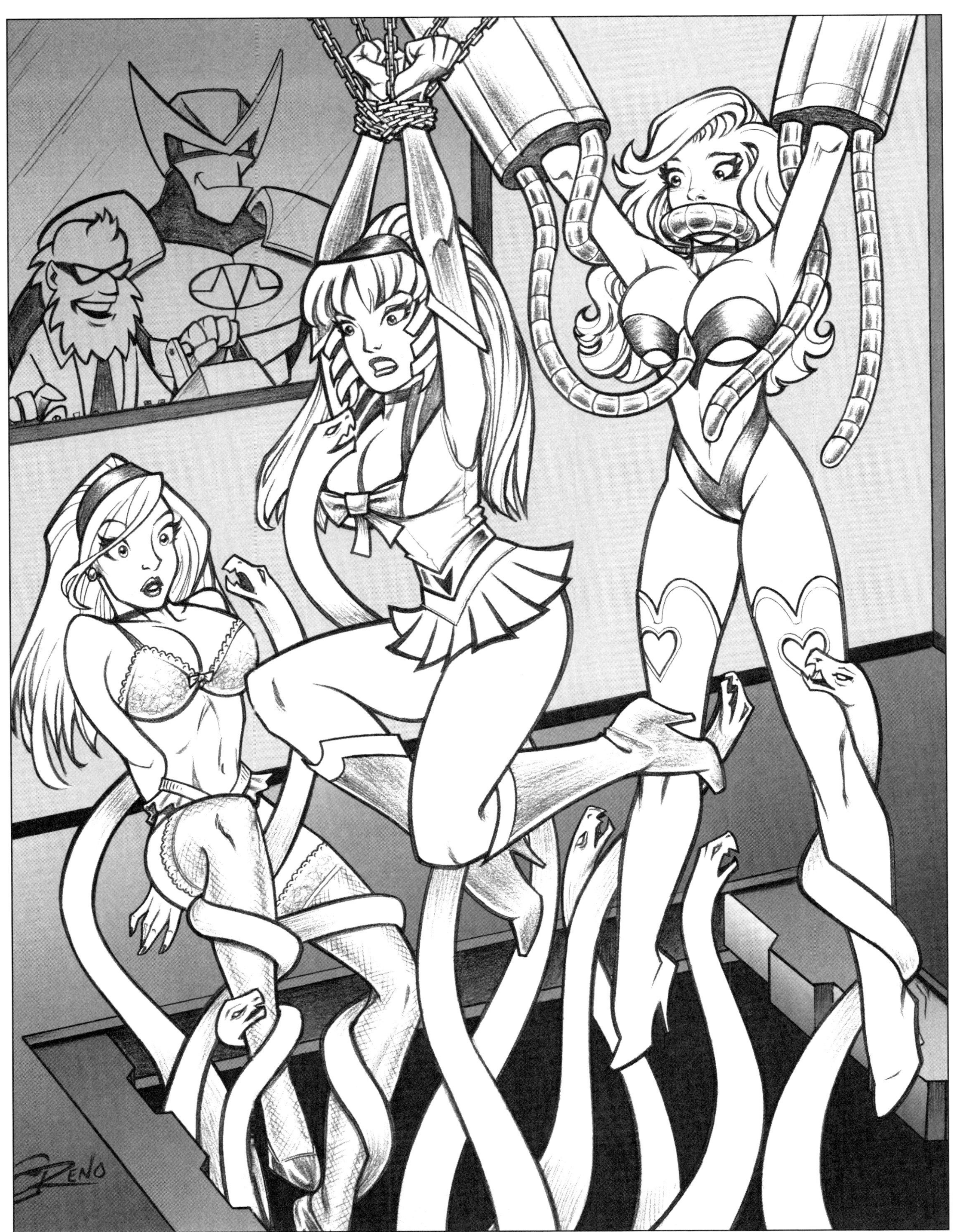

*BOUND vs GAGGS*

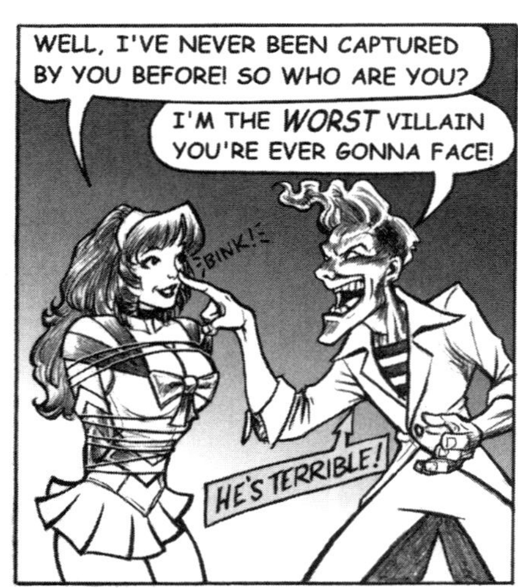
WELL, I'VE NEVER BEEN CAPTURED BY YOU BEFORE! SO WHO ARE YOU?
I'M THE WORST VILLAIN YOU'RE EVER GONNA FACE!
BINK!
HE'S TERRIBLE!

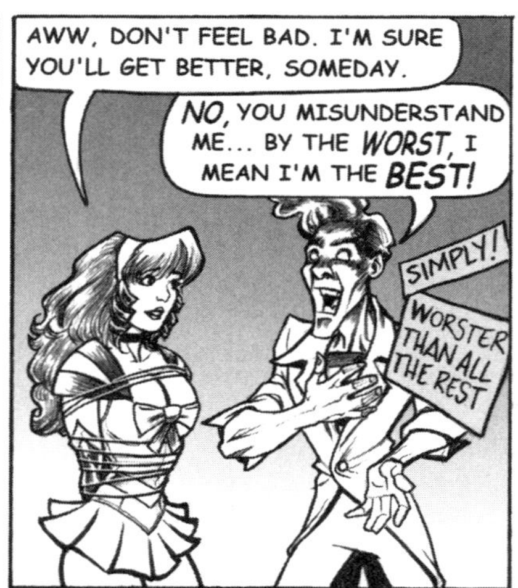
AWW, DON'T FEEL BAD. I'M SURE YOU'LL GET BETTER, SOMEDAY.
NO, YOU MISUNDERSTAND ME... BY THE WORST, I MEAN I'M THE BEST!
SIMPLY!
WORSTER THAN ALL THE REST

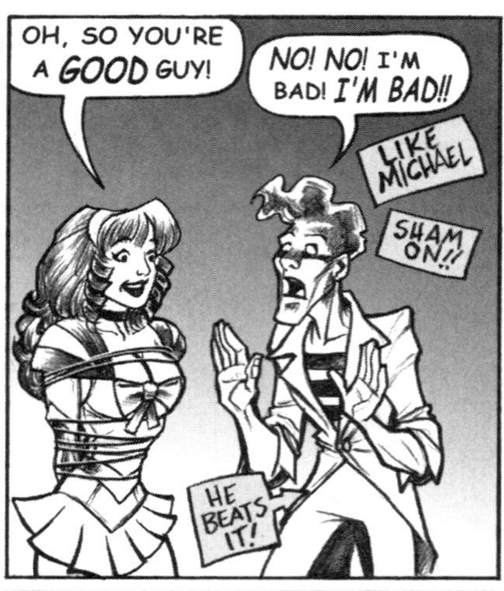
OH, SO YOU'RE A GOOD GUY!
NO! NO! I'M BAD! I'M BAD!!
LIKE MICHAEL
SHAM ON!!
HE BEATS IT!

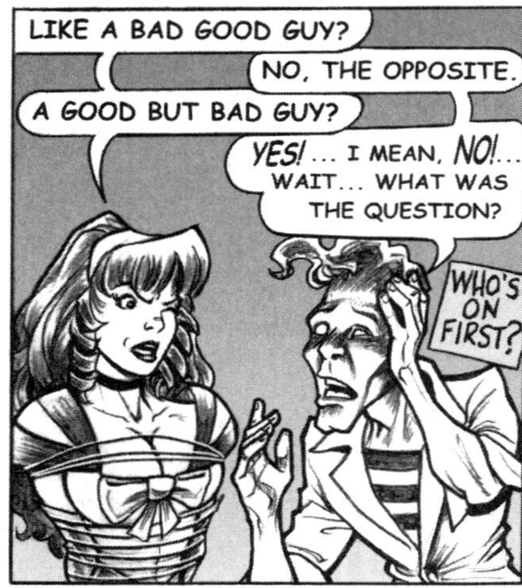
LIKE A BAD GOOD GUY?
NO, THE OPPOSITE.
A GOOD BUT BAD GUY?
YES! ... I MEAN, NO!... WAIT... WHAT WAS THE QUESTION?
WHO'S ON FIRST?

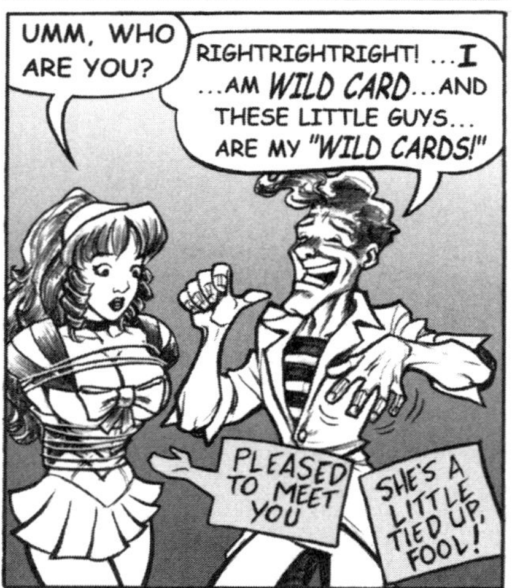
UMM, WHO ARE YOU?
RIGHTRIGHTRIGHT! ...I ...AM WILD CARD...AND THESE LITTLE GUYS... ARE MY "WILD CARDS!"
PLEASED TO MEET YOU
SHE'S A LITTLE TIED UP, FOOL!

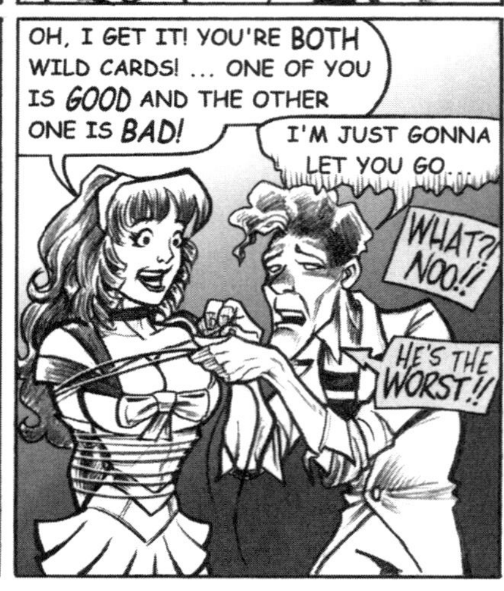
OH, I GET IT! YOU'RE BOTH WILD CARDS! ... ONE OF YOU IS GOOD AND THE OTHER ONE IS BAD!
I'M JUST GONNA LET YOU GO...
WHAT?! NOO!!
HE'S THE WORST!!

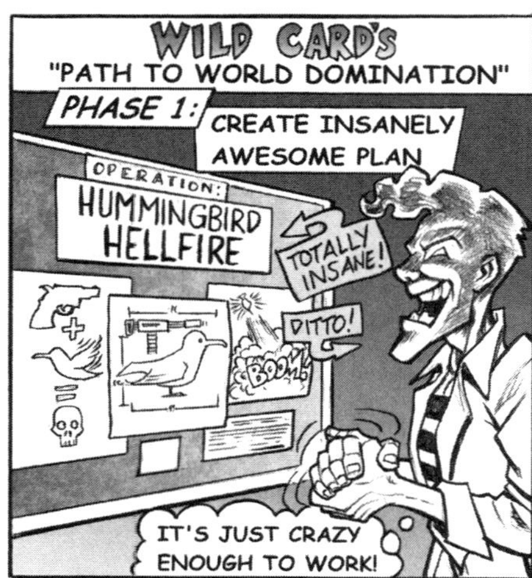
WILD CARD'S
"PATH TO WORLD DOMINATION"
PHASE 1:
CREATE INSANELY AWESOME PLAN
OPERATION:
HUMMINGBIRD HELLFIRE
TOTALLY INSANE!
DITTO!
BOOM!
IT'S JUST CRAZY ENOUGH TO WORK!

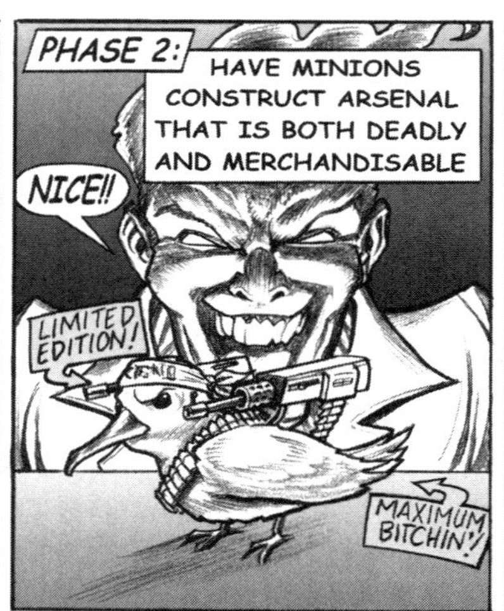
PHASE 2:
HAVE MINIONS CONSTRUCT ARSENAL THAT IS BOTH DEADLY AND MERCHANDISABLE
NICE!!
LIMITED EDITION!
MAXIMUM BITCHIN'!

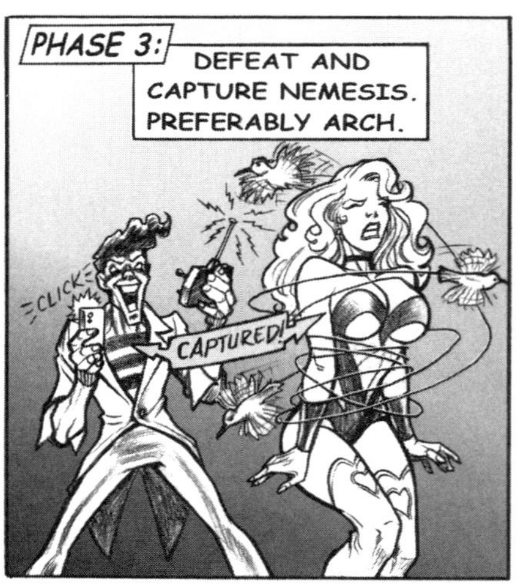
PHASE 3:
DEFEAT AND CAPTURE NEMESIS. PREFERABLY ARCH.
CLICK
CAPTURED!

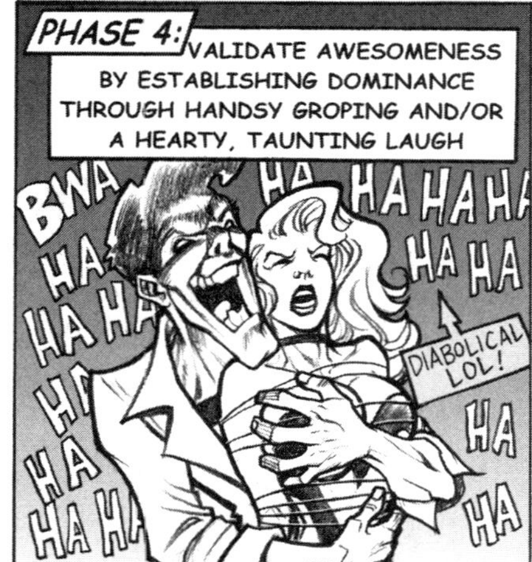
PHASE 4:
VALIDATE AWESOMENESS BY ESTABLISHING DOMINANCE THROUGH HANDSY GROPING AND/OR A HEARTY, TAUNTING LAUGH
BWA HA HA HA HA HA HA HA HA HA HA HA HA HA HA HA
DIABOLICAL LOL!

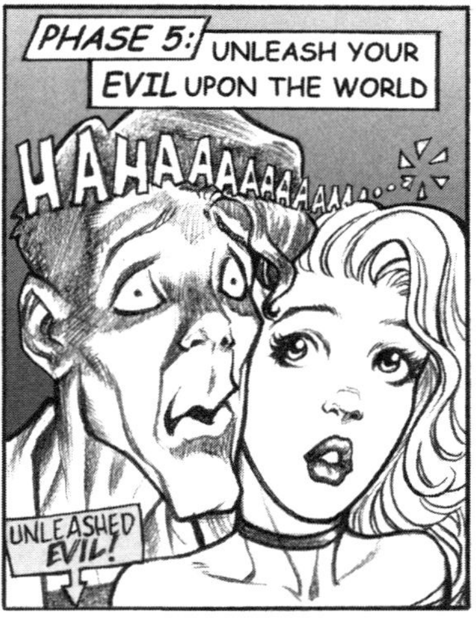
PHASE 5:
UNLEASH YOUR EVIL UPON THE WORLD
HAHAAAAAAAAAA...
UNLEASHED EVIL!

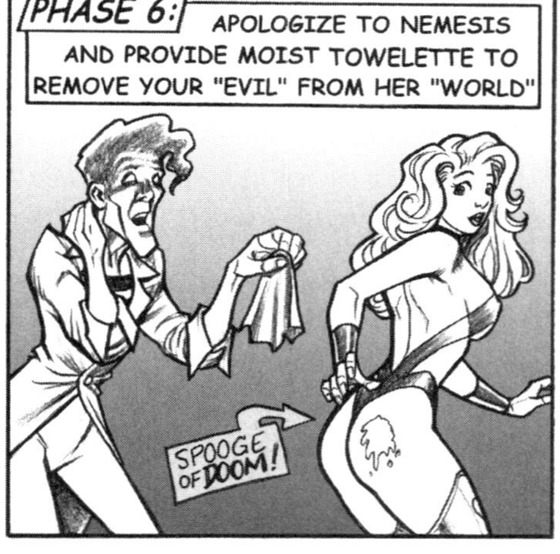
PHASE 6:
APOLOGIZE TO NEMESIS AND PROVIDE MOIST TOWELETTE TO REMOVE YOUR "EVIL" FROM HER "WORLD"
SPOOGE OF DOOM!

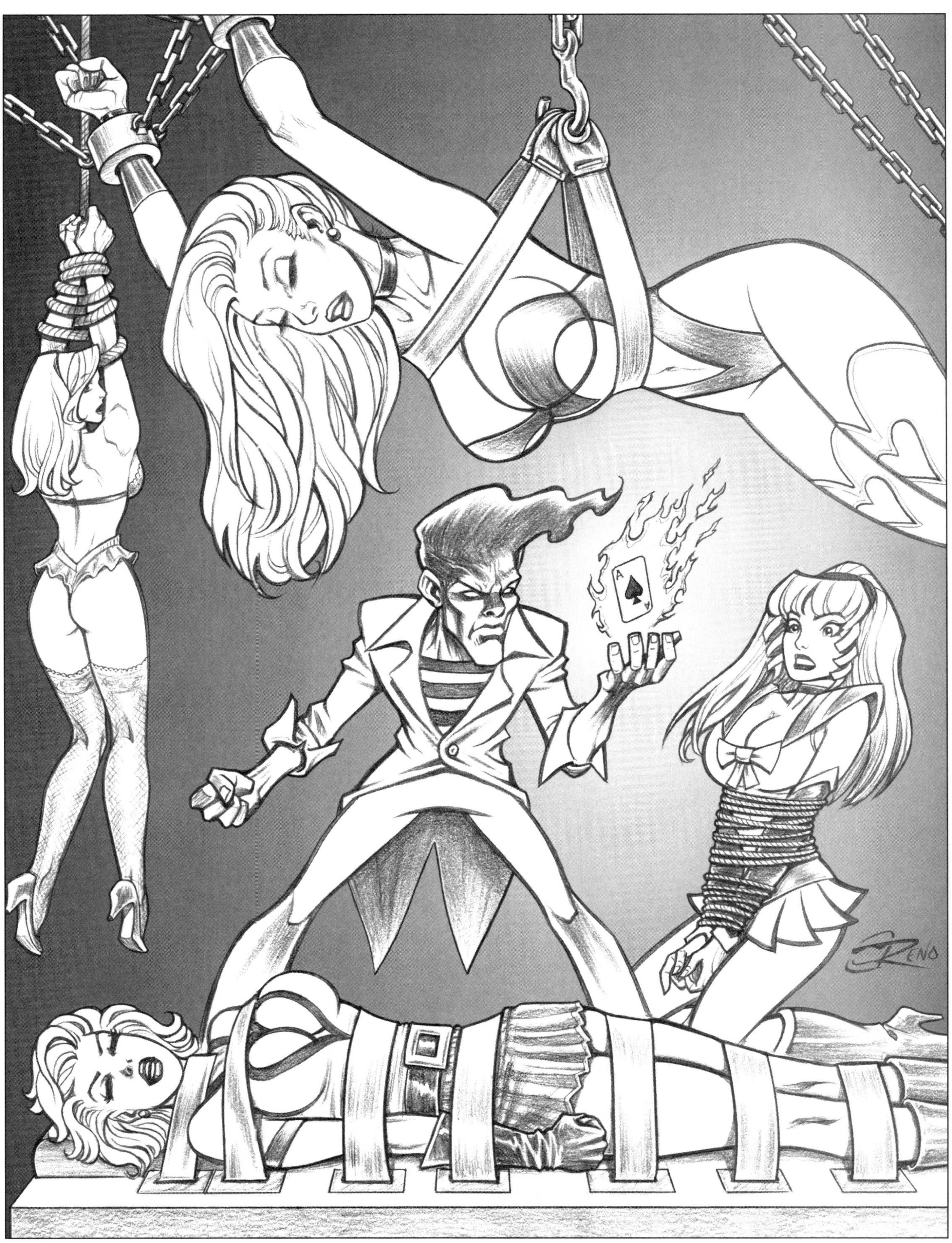

*Time Frame*

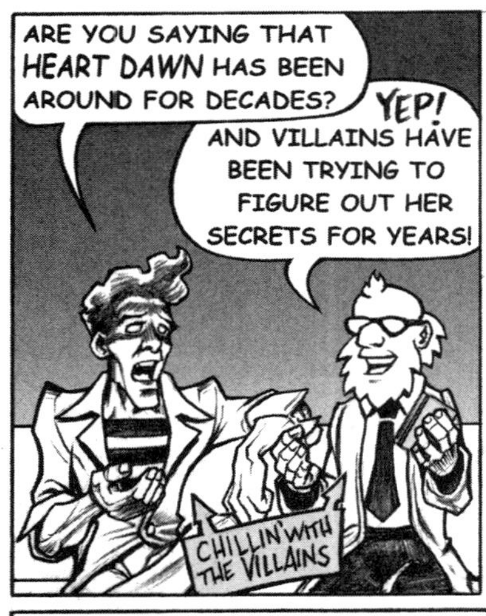
ARE YOU SAYING THAT HEART DAWN HAS BEEN AROUND FOR DECADES?
YEP!
AND VILLAINS HAVE BEEN TRYING TO FIGURE OUT HER SECRETS FOR YEARS!
CHILLIN' WITH THE VILLAINS

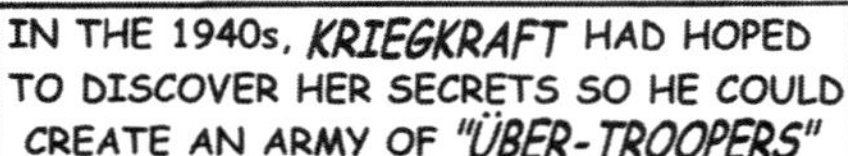
IN THE 1940s, KRIEGKRAFT HAD HOPED TO DISCOVER HER SECRETS SO HE COULD CREATE AN ARMY OF "ÜBER-TROOPERS"

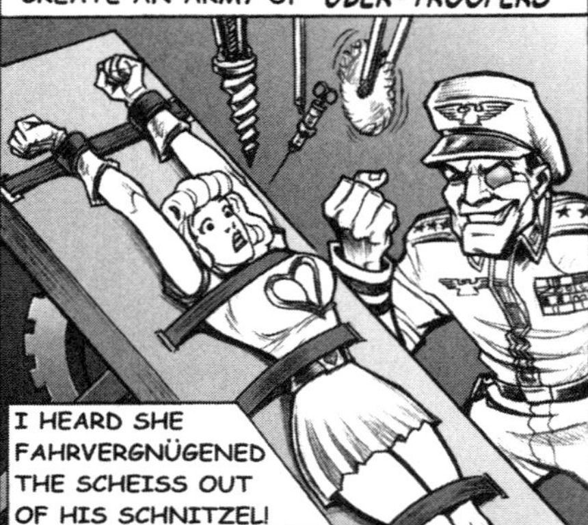
I HEARD SHE FAHRVERGNÜGENED THE SCHEISS OUT OF HIS SCHNITZEL!

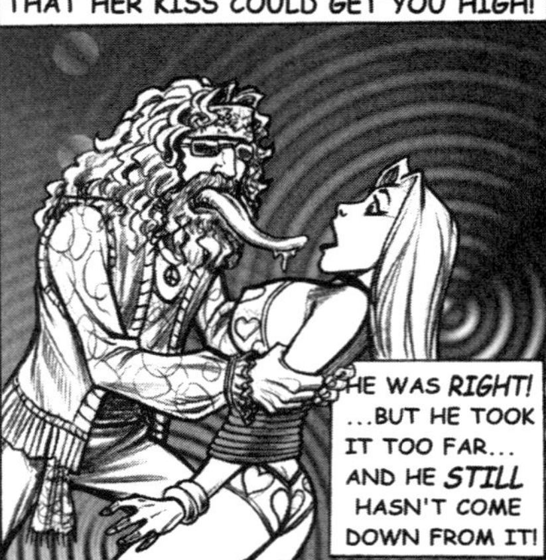
IN THE 1960s, PSYCHO-DELIC HEARD THAT HER KISS COULD GET YOU HIGH!
HE WAS RIGHT! ...BUT HE TOOK IT TOO FAR... AND HE STILL HASN'T COME DOWN FROM IT!

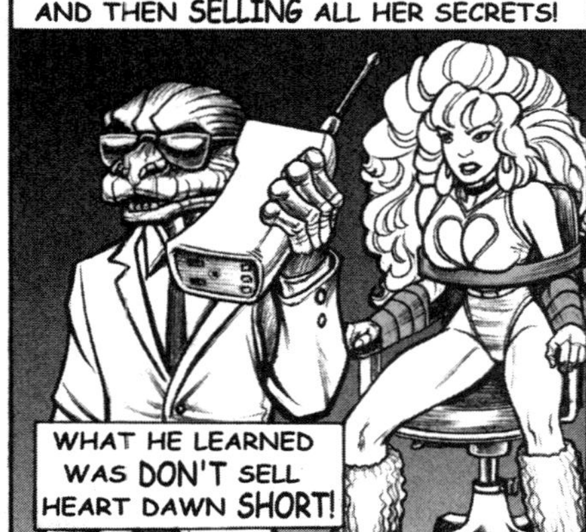
IN THE 1980s, GREEDY GECKO BELIEVED HE COULD MAKE BILLIONS BY LEARNING AND THEN SELLING ALL HER SECRETS!
WHAT HE LEARNED WAS DON'T SELL HEART DAWN SHORT!

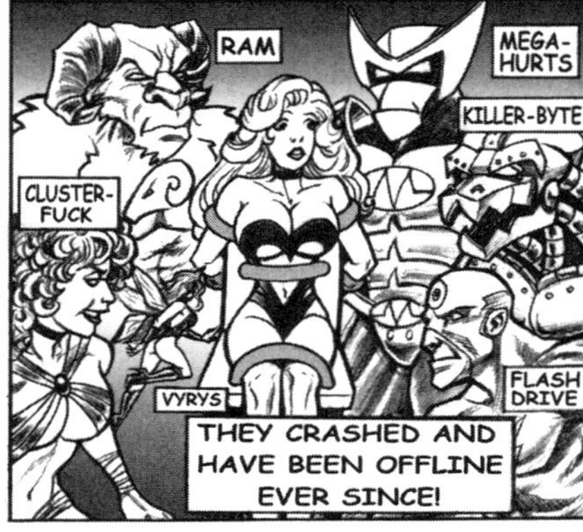
IN THE 2000s, THE CYBER-SIX FELT THEY HAD THE TECHNICAL KNOW HOW TO FINALLY GET SOME ANSWERS!
RAM
MEGA-HURTS
KILLER-BYTE
CLUSTER-FUCK
VYRYS
FLASH DRIVE
THEY CRASHED AND HAVE BEEN OFFLINE EVER SINCE!

SO YOU HAVE "HEART DAWN IN PERIL" TRADING CARDS?
ALL 7,800 OF THEM!
LOOK HOW YOUNG MEGA-HURTS LOOKS IN THIS ONE!
CAPTURE THEM ALL!

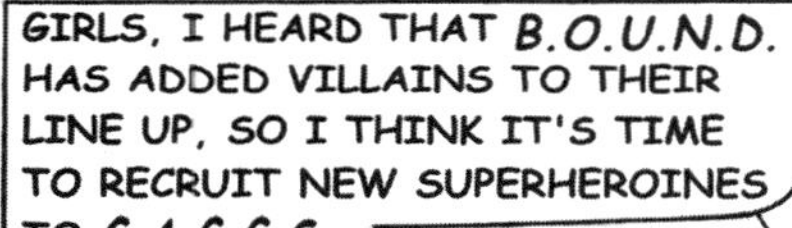
GIRLS, I HEARD THAT B.O.U.N.D. HAS ADDED VILLAINS TO THEIR LINE UP, SO I THINK IT'S TIME TO RECRUIT NEW SUPERHEROINES TO G.A.G.G.S.

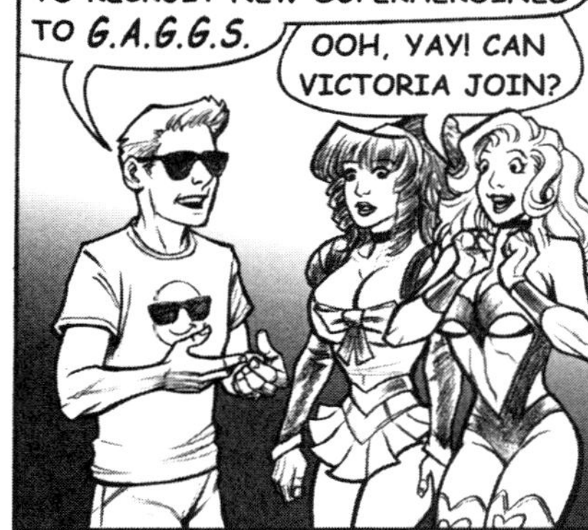
OOH, YAY! CAN VICTORIA JOIN?

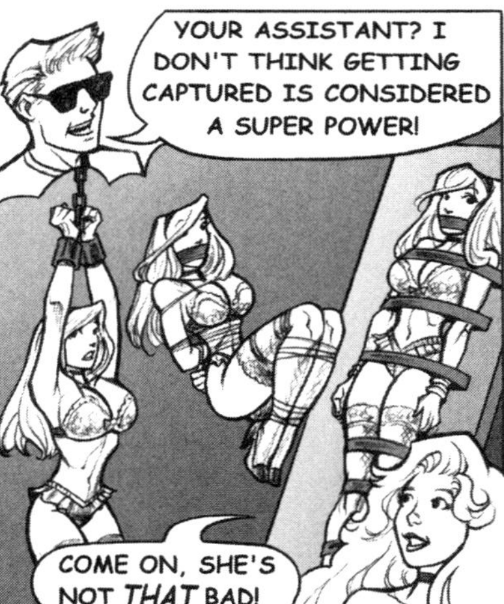
YOUR ASSISTANT? I DON'T THINK GETTING CAPTURED IS CONSIDERED A SUPER POWER!
COME ON, SHE'S NOT THAT BAD!

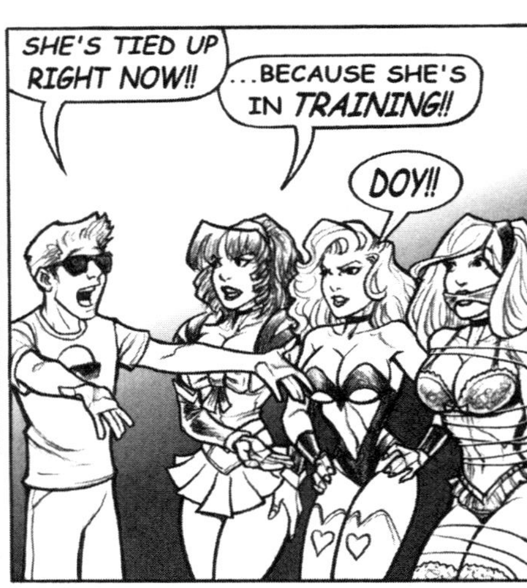
SHE'S TIED UP RIGHT NOW!!
...BECAUSE SHE'S IN TRAINING!!
DOY!!

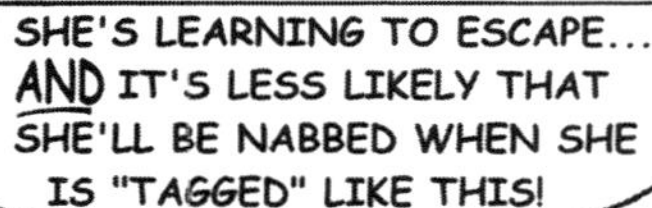
SHE'S LEARNING TO ESCAPE... AND IT'S LESS LIKELY THAT SHE'LL BE NABBED WHEN SHE IS "TAGGED" LIKE THIS!

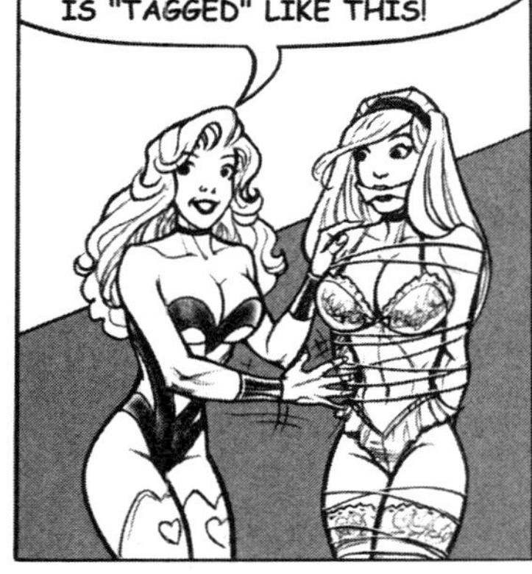

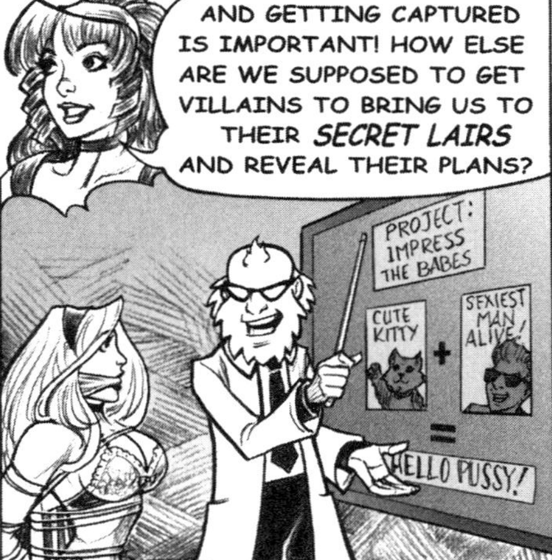
AND GETTING CAPTURED IS IMPORTANT! HOW ELSE ARE WE SUPPOSED TO GET VILLAINS TO BRING US TO THEIR SECRET LAIRS AND REVEAL THEIR PLANS?
PROJECT: IMPRESS THE BABES
CUTE KITTY
SEXIEST MAN ALIVE!
HELLO PUSSY!

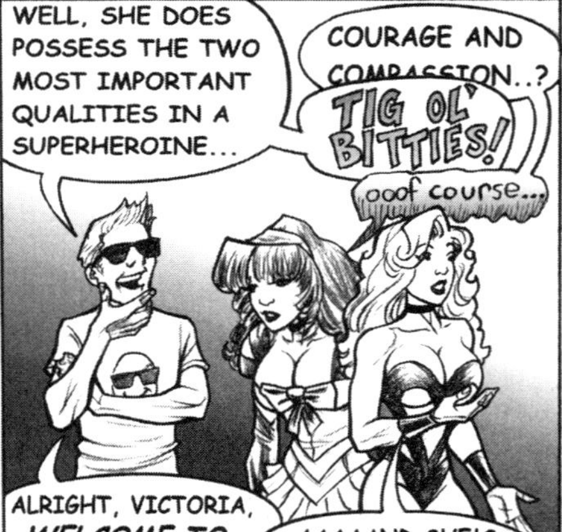
WELL, SHE DOES POSSESS THE TWO MOST IMPORTANT QUALITIES IN A SUPERHEROINE...
COURAGE AND COMPASSION..?
TIG OL' BITTIES!
oooof course...
ALRIGHT, VICTORIA, WELCOME TO G.A.G.G.S.!!
...AAAAAND SHE'S BEEN CAPTURED!

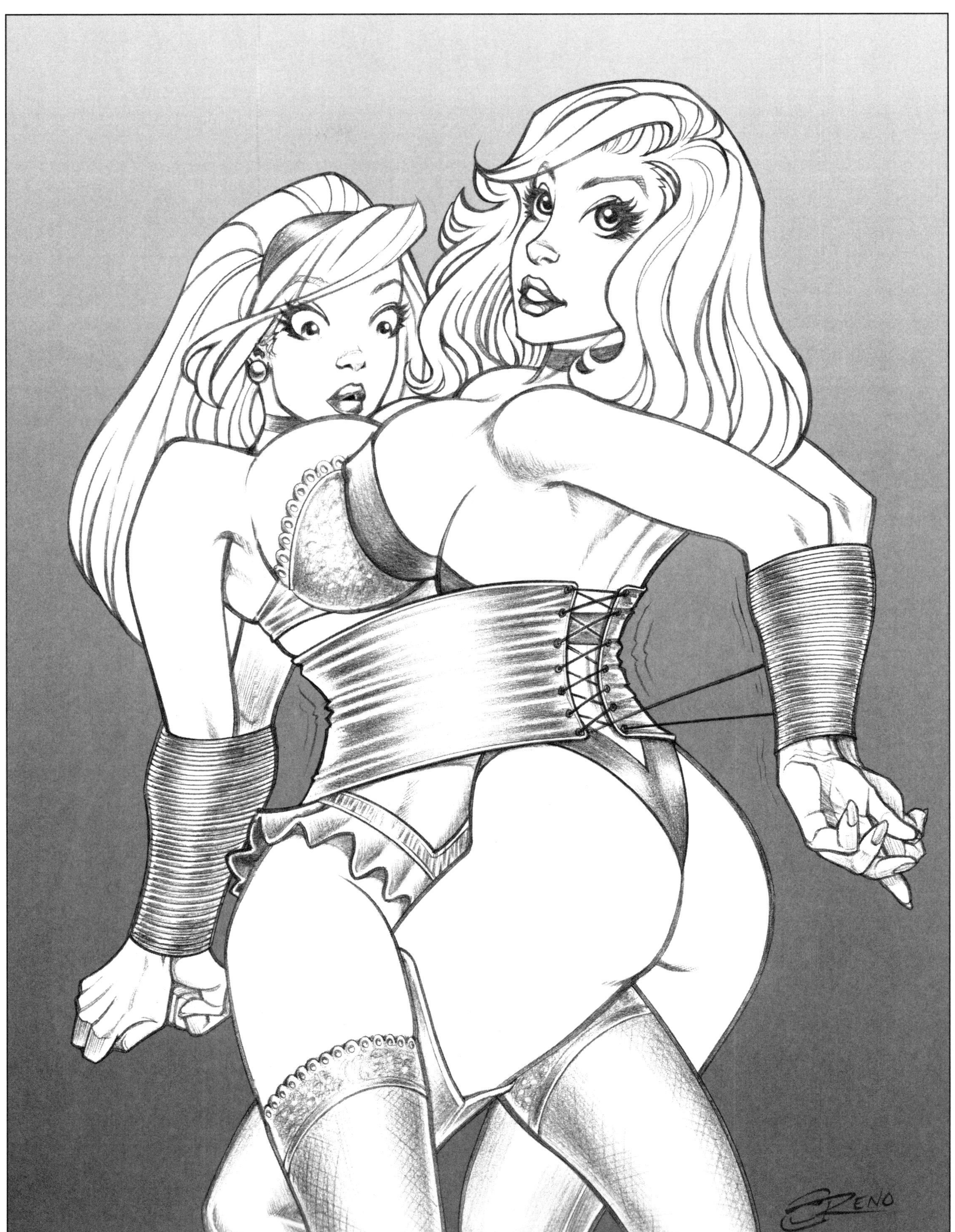

*Collision Corset*

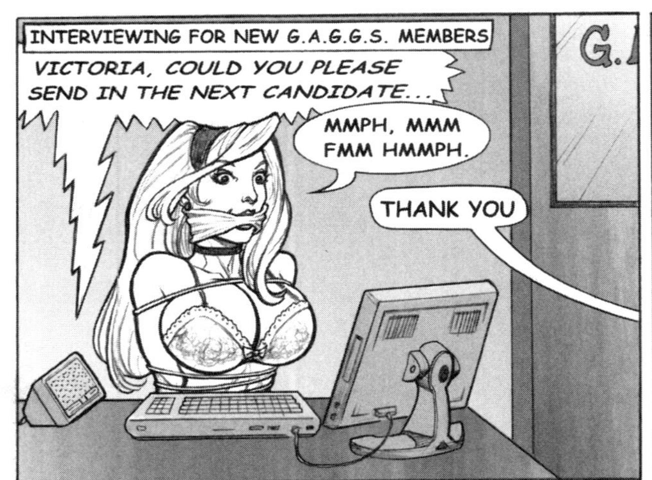
INTERVIEWING FOR NEW G.A.G.G.S. MEMBERS
VICTORIA, COULD YOU PLEASE SEND IN THE NEXT CANDIDATE...
MMPH, MMM FMM HMMPH.
THANK YOU

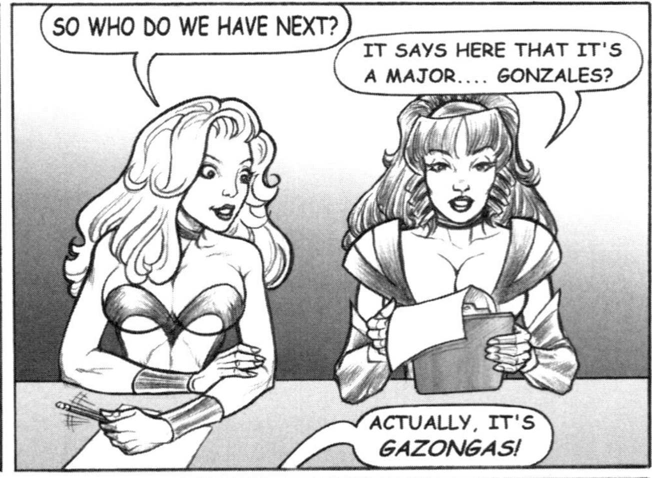
SO WHO DO WE HAVE NEXT?
IT SAYS HERE THAT IT'S A MAJOR.... GONZALES?
ACTUALLY, IT'S GAZONGAS!

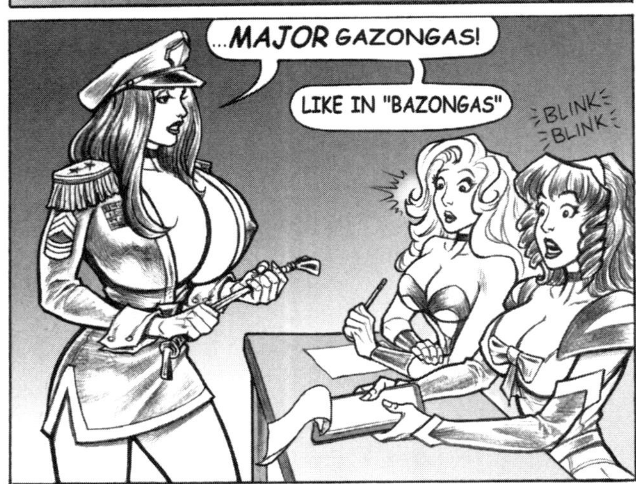
...MAJOR GAZONGAS!
LIKE IN "BAZONGAS"
BLINK BLINK

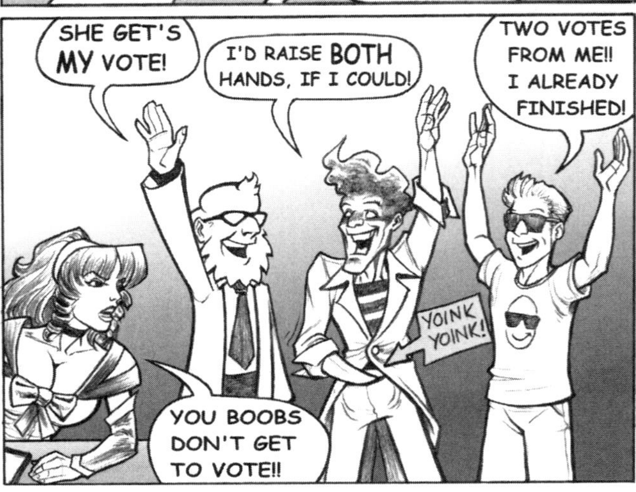
SHE GET'S MY VOTE!
I'D RAISE BOTH HANDS, IF I COULD!
TWO VOTES FROM ME!! I ALREADY FINISHED!
YOINK YOINK!
YOU BOOBS DON'T GET TO VOTE!!

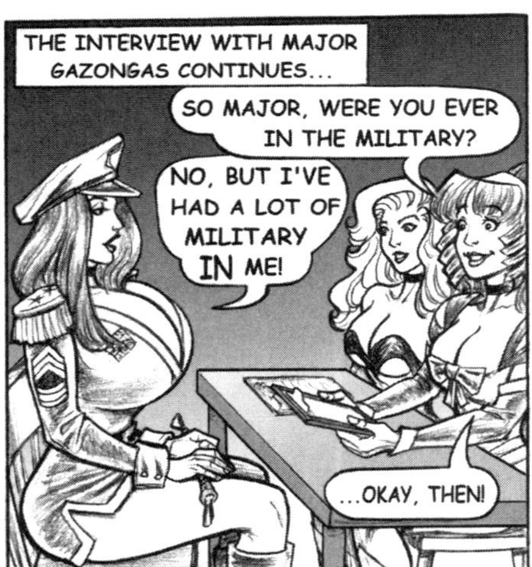
THE INTERVIEW WITH MAJOR GAZONGAS CONTINUES...
SO MAJOR, WERE YOU EVER IN THE MILITARY?
NO, BUT I'VE HAD A LOT OF MILITARY IN ME!
...OKAY, THEN!

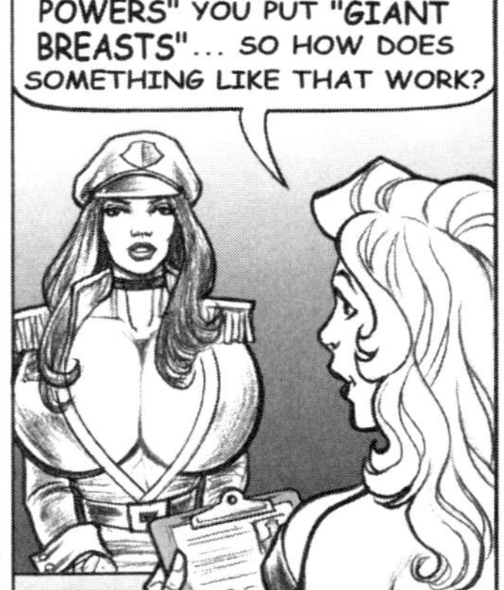
I NOTICED UNDER "SUPER POWERS" YOU PUT "GIANT BREASTS"... SO HOW DOES SOMETHING LIKE THAT WORK?

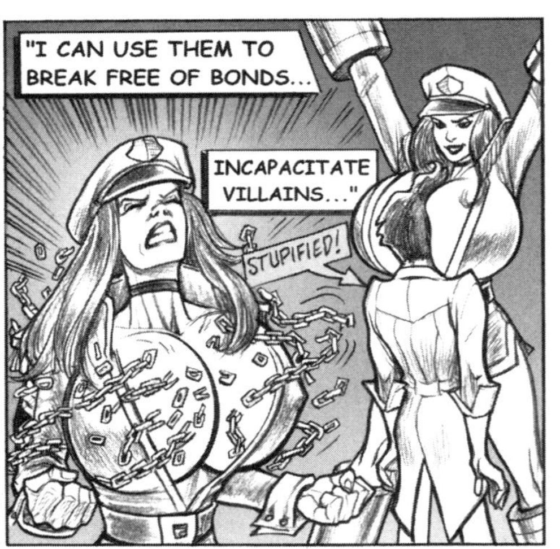
"I CAN USE THEM TO BREAK FREE OF BONDS...
INCAPACITATE VILLAINS..."
STUPIFIED!

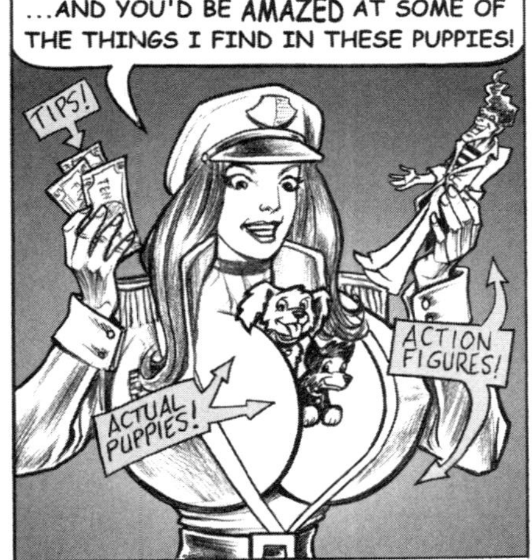
...AND YOU'D BE AMAZED AT SOME OF THE THINGS I FIND IN THESE PUPPIES!
TIPS!
ACTION FIGURES!
ACTUAL PUPPIES!

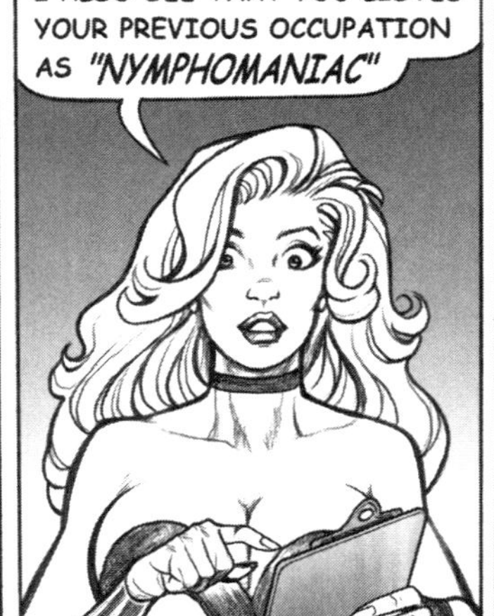
I ALSO SEE THAT YOU LISTED YOUR PREVIOUS OCCUPATION AS "NYMPHOMANIAC"

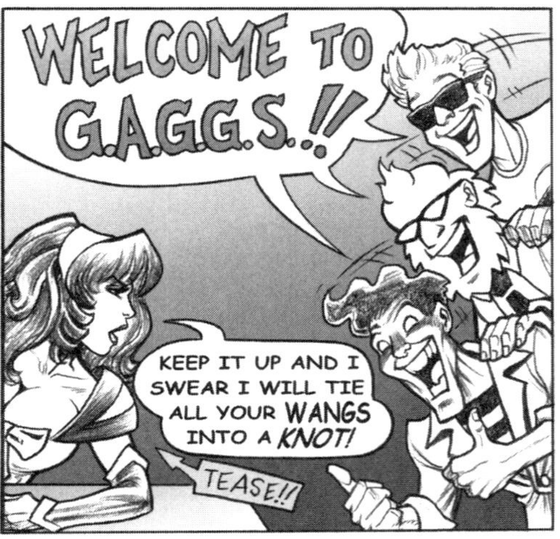
WELCOME TO G.A.G.G.S.!!
KEEP IT UP AND I SWEAR I WILL TIE ALL YOUR WANGS INTO A KNOT!
TEASE!!

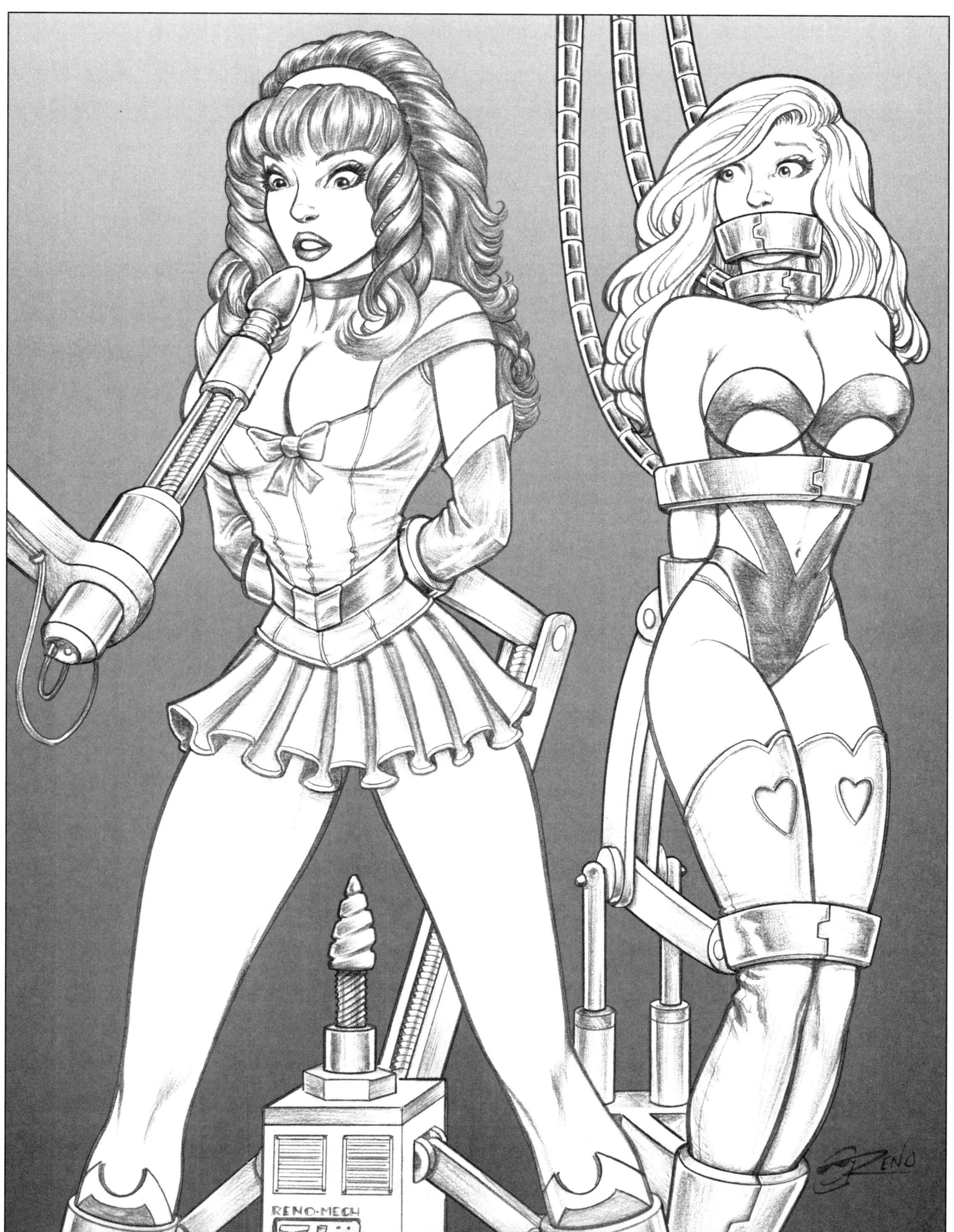


*GAGGS CosPlayers*

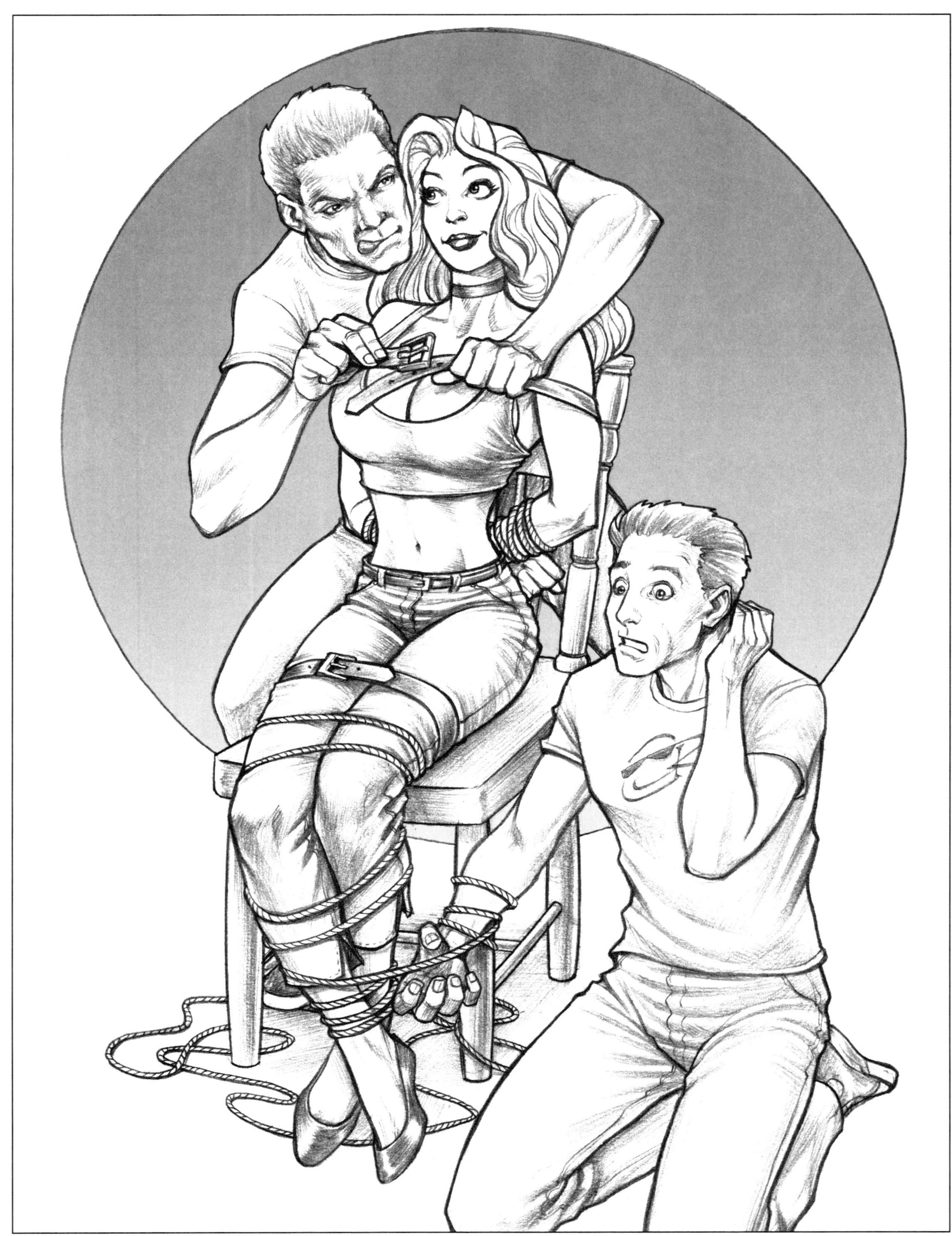

*Minion Camp*

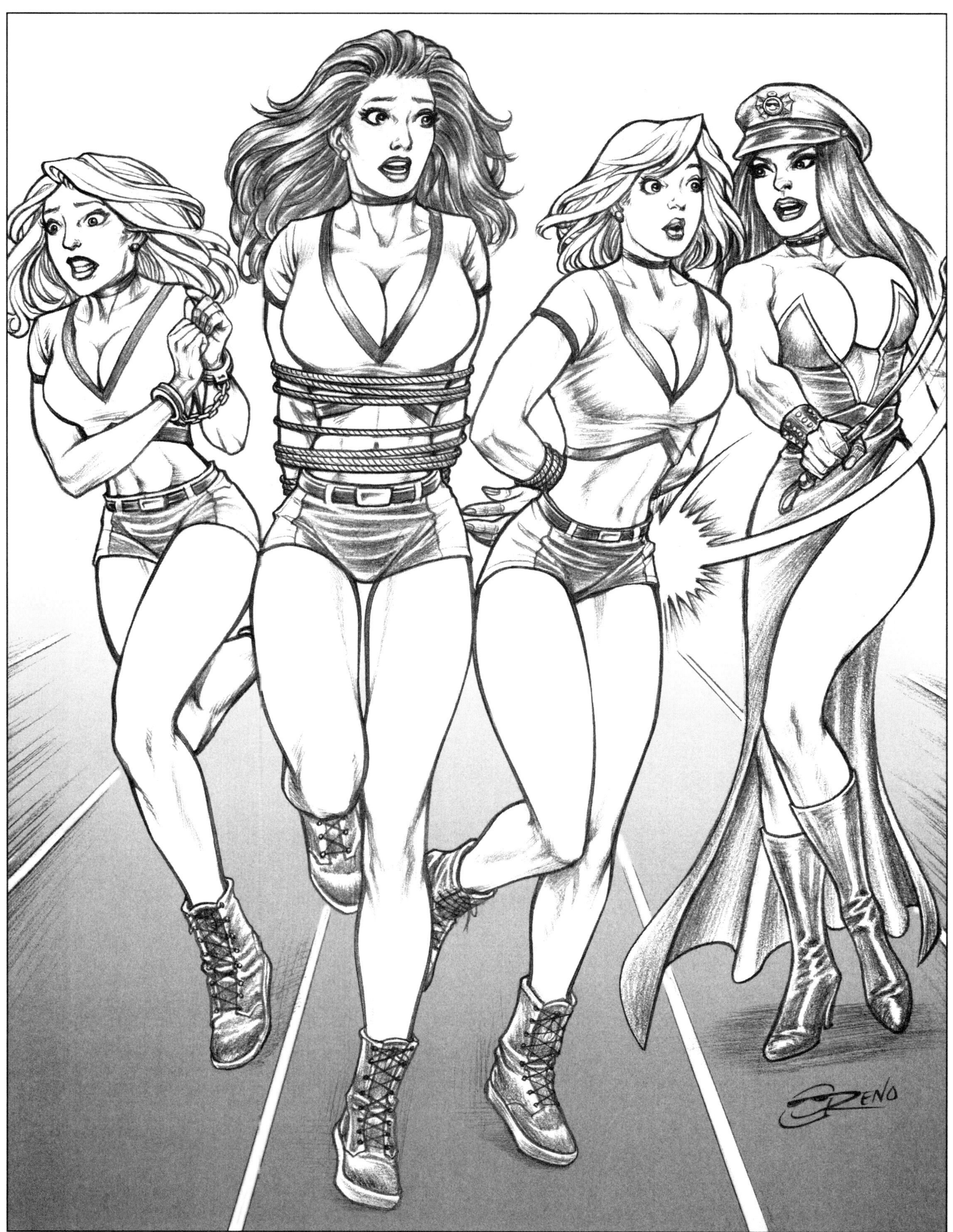

*Basic Restraining*

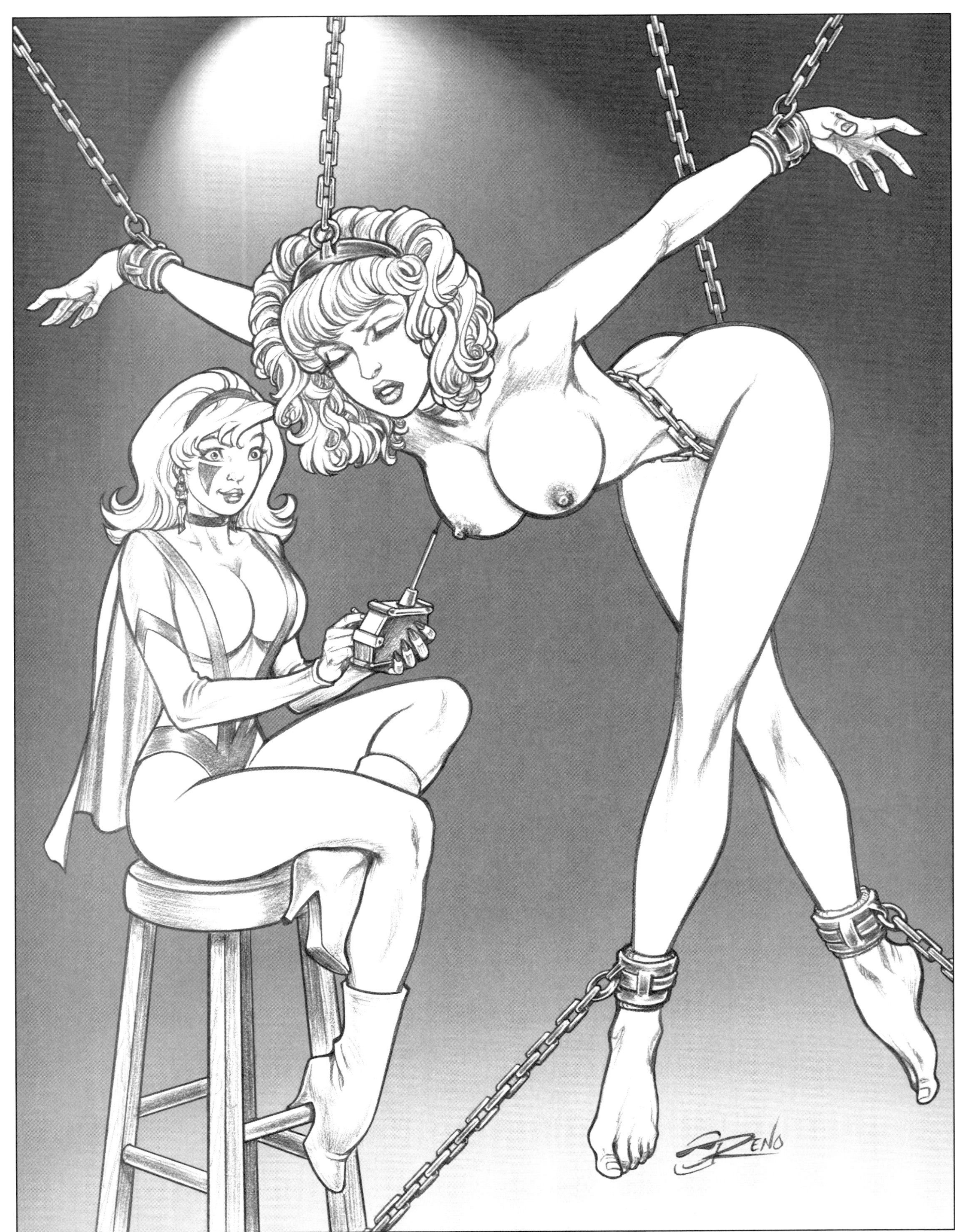


*Marie -Annette*

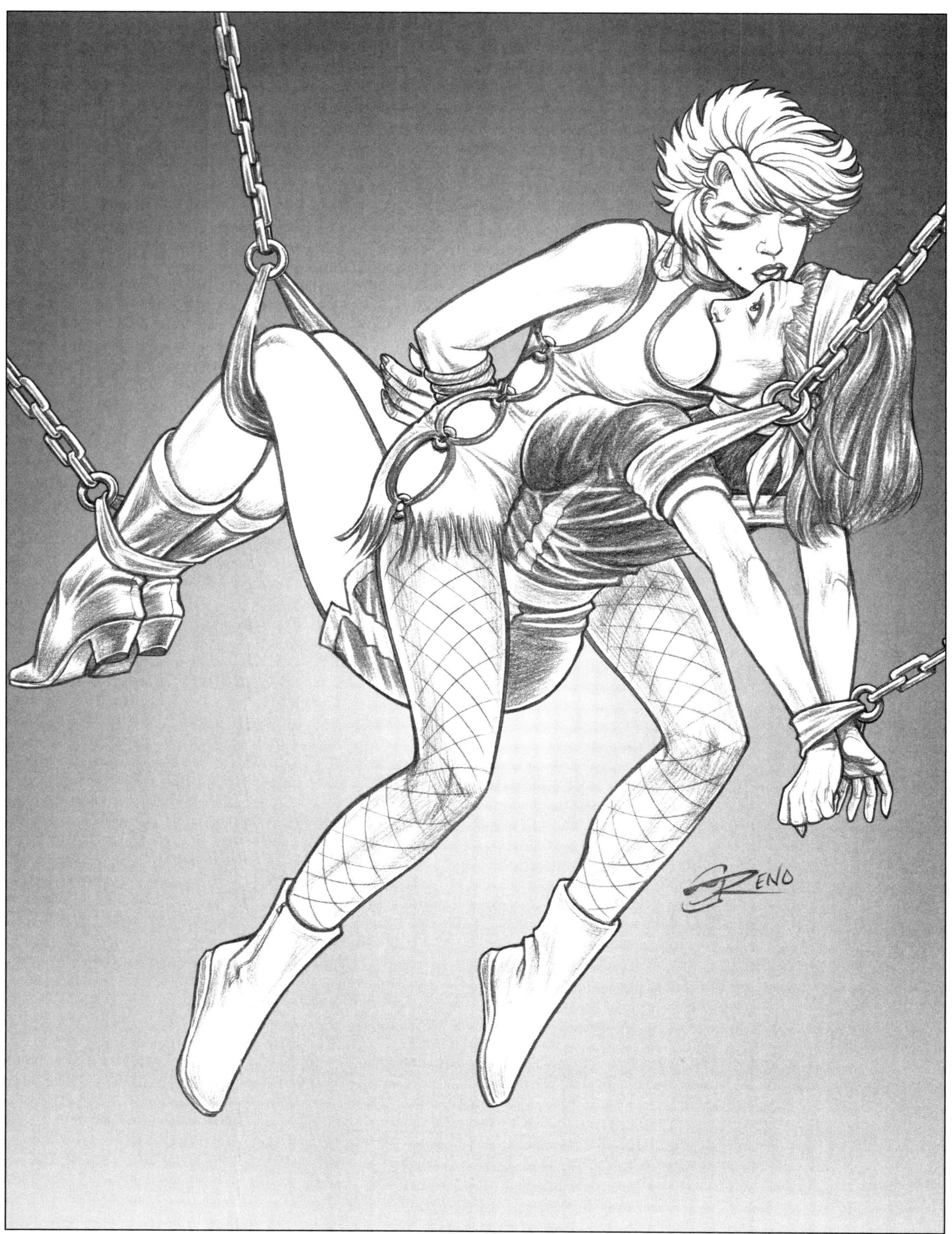


*Swingers*

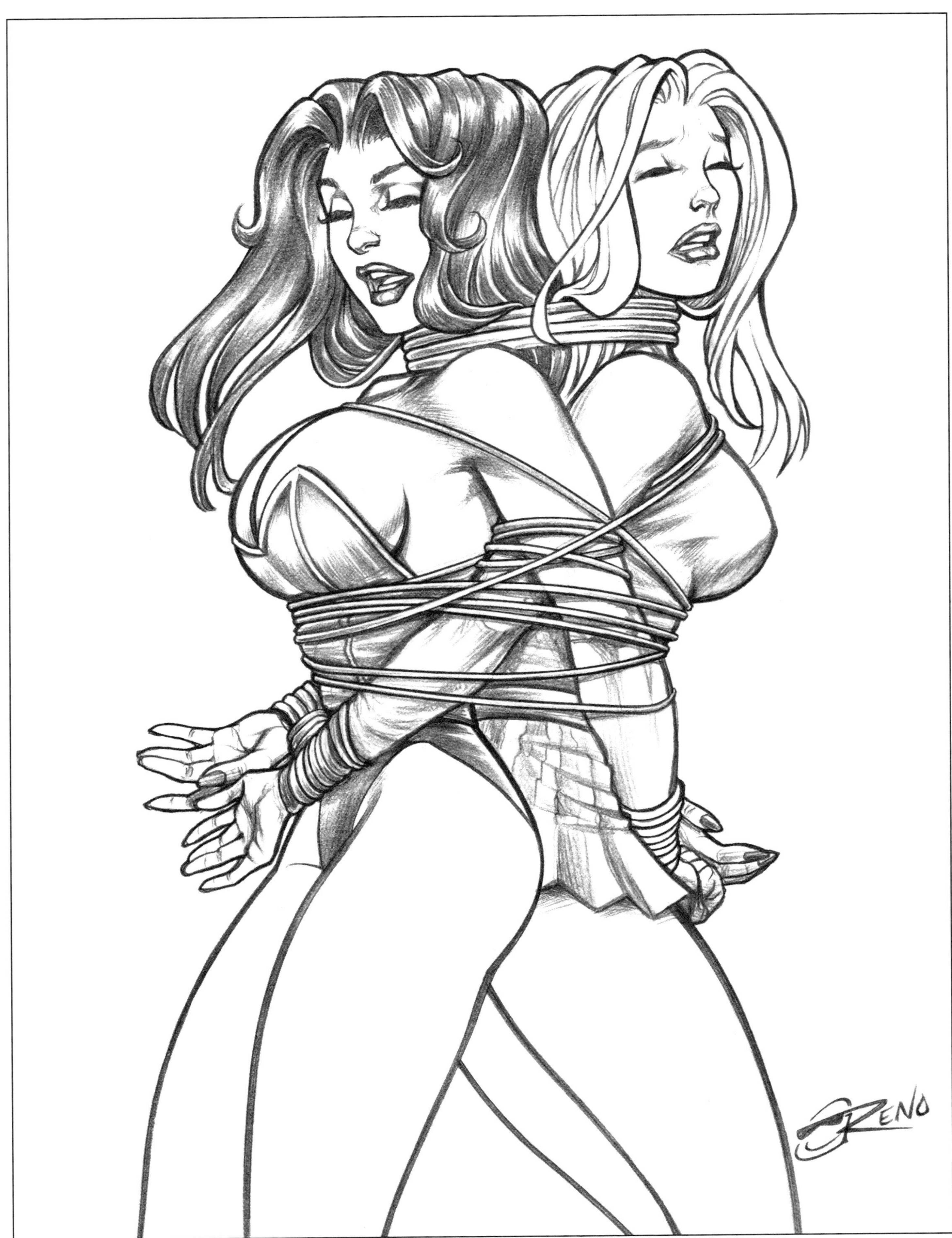

*Back Up*

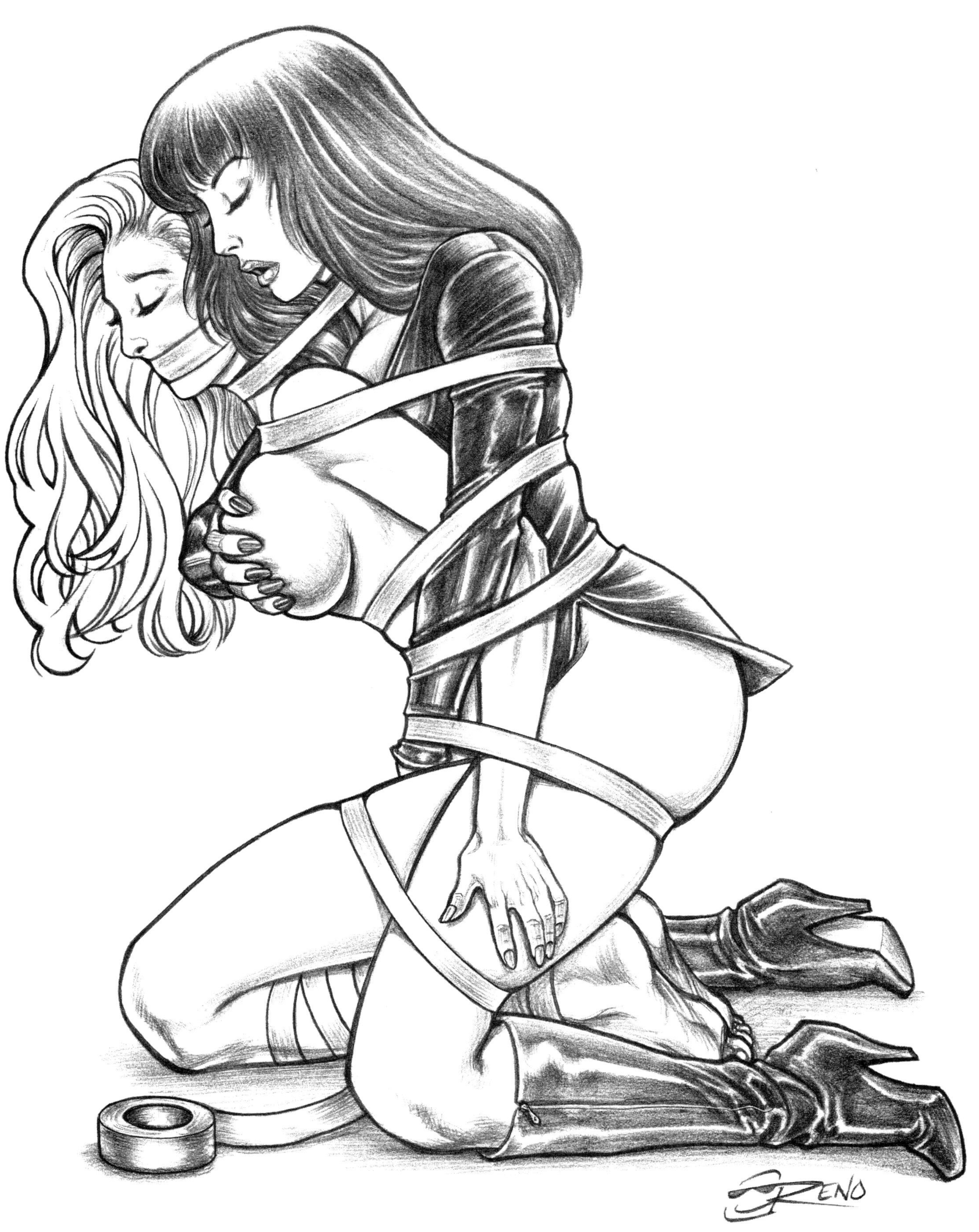

*Duct and Covered*

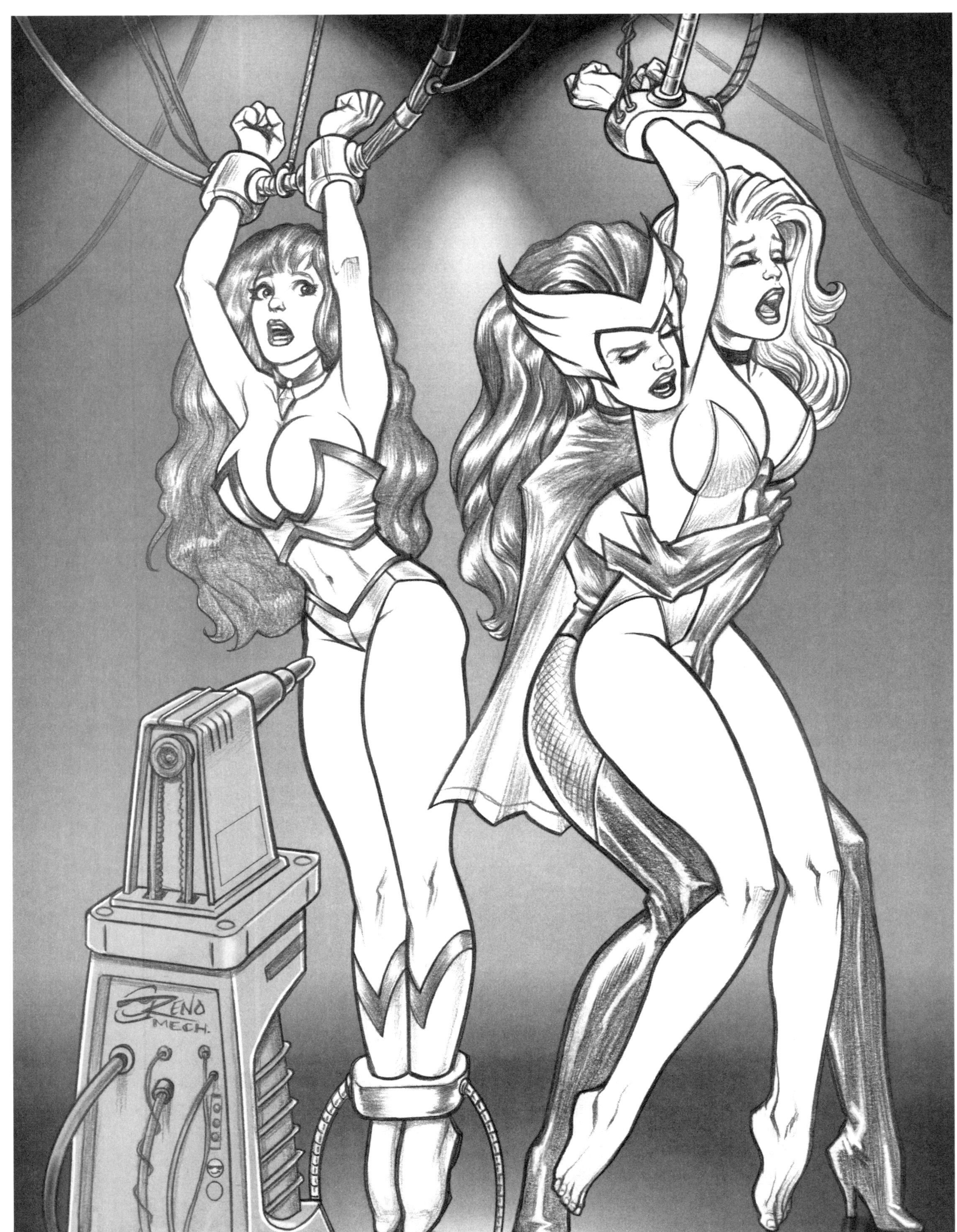


*In the Hands of the Bird*

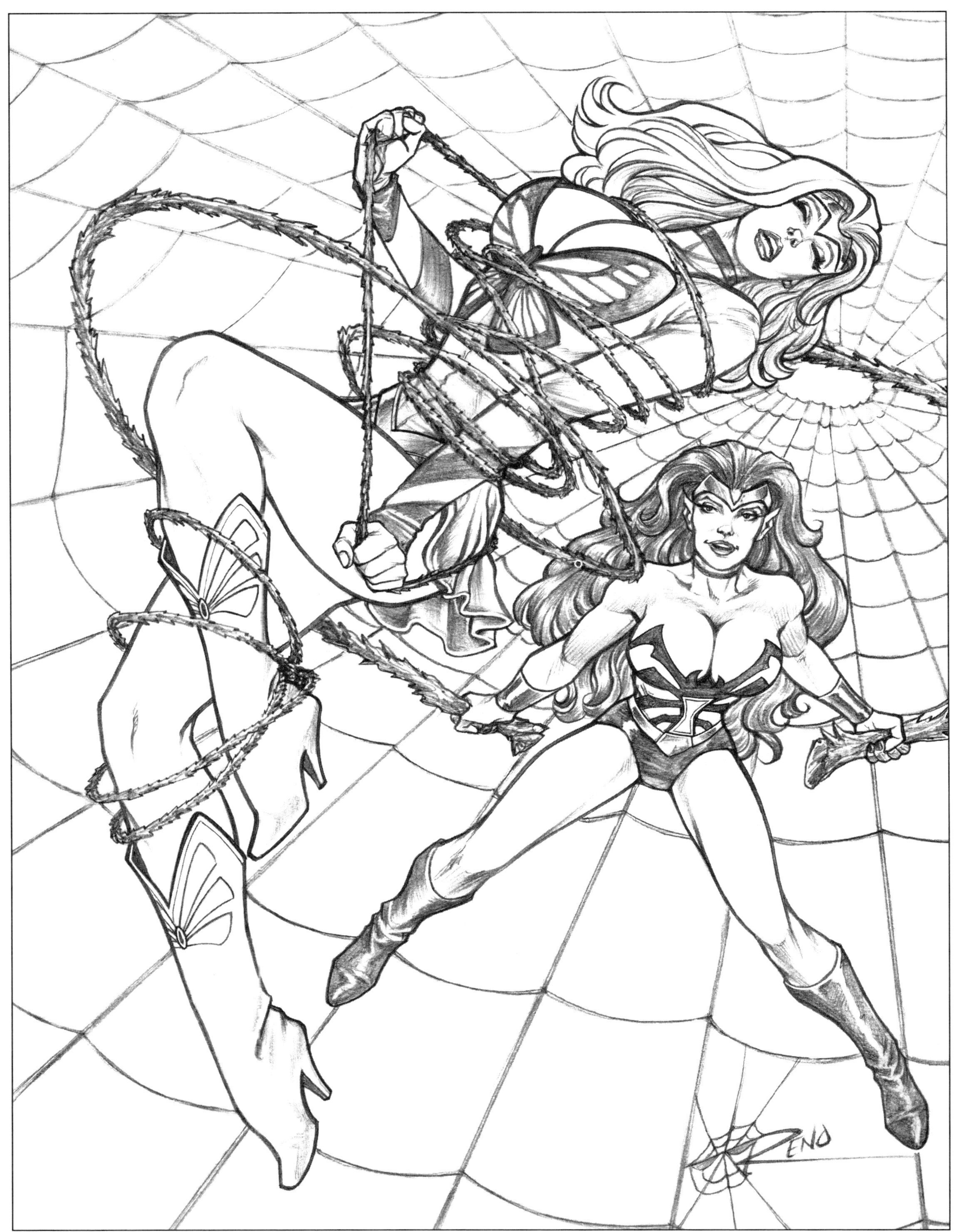

*In the Web of the Widow*

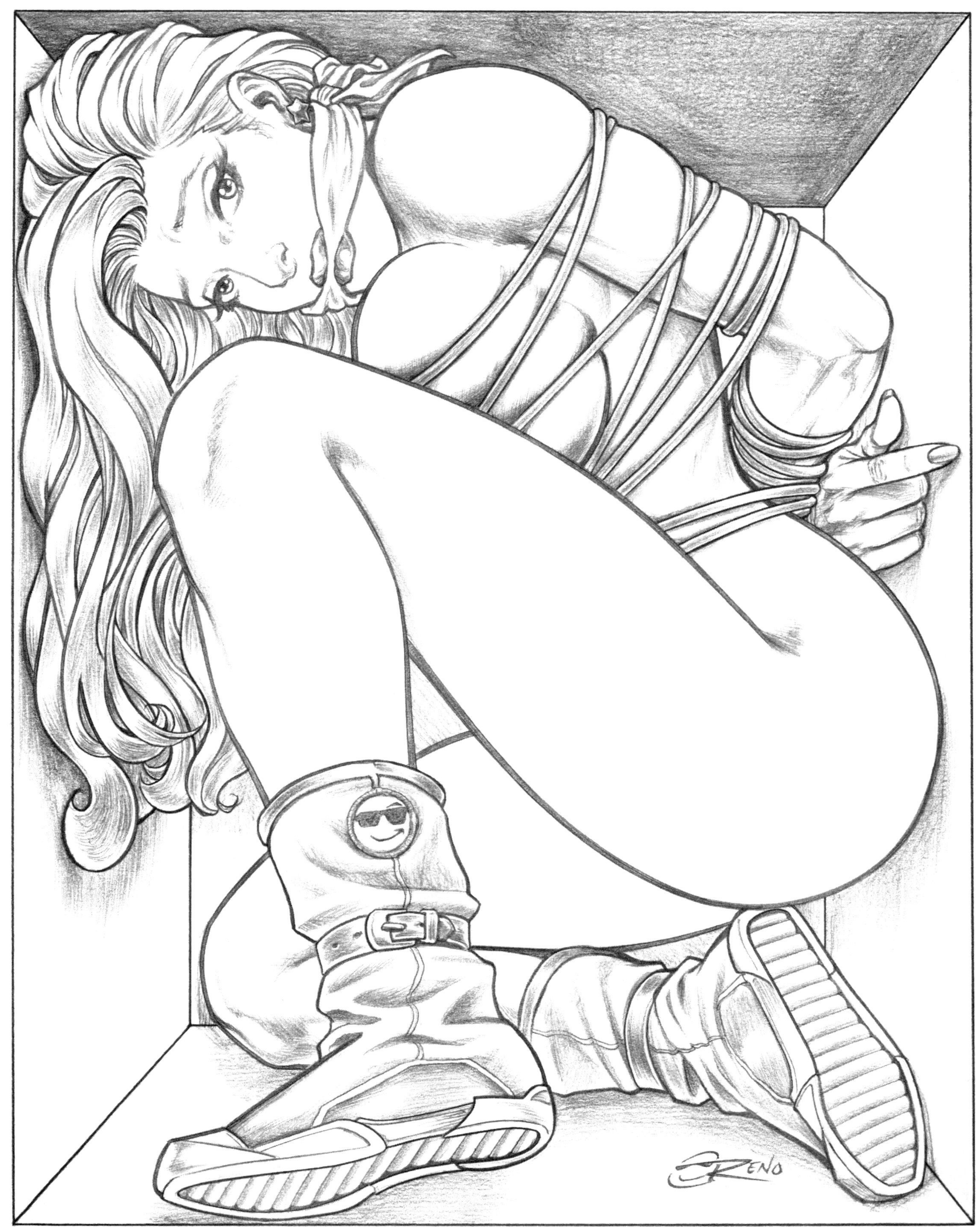

*Box Set CD1*

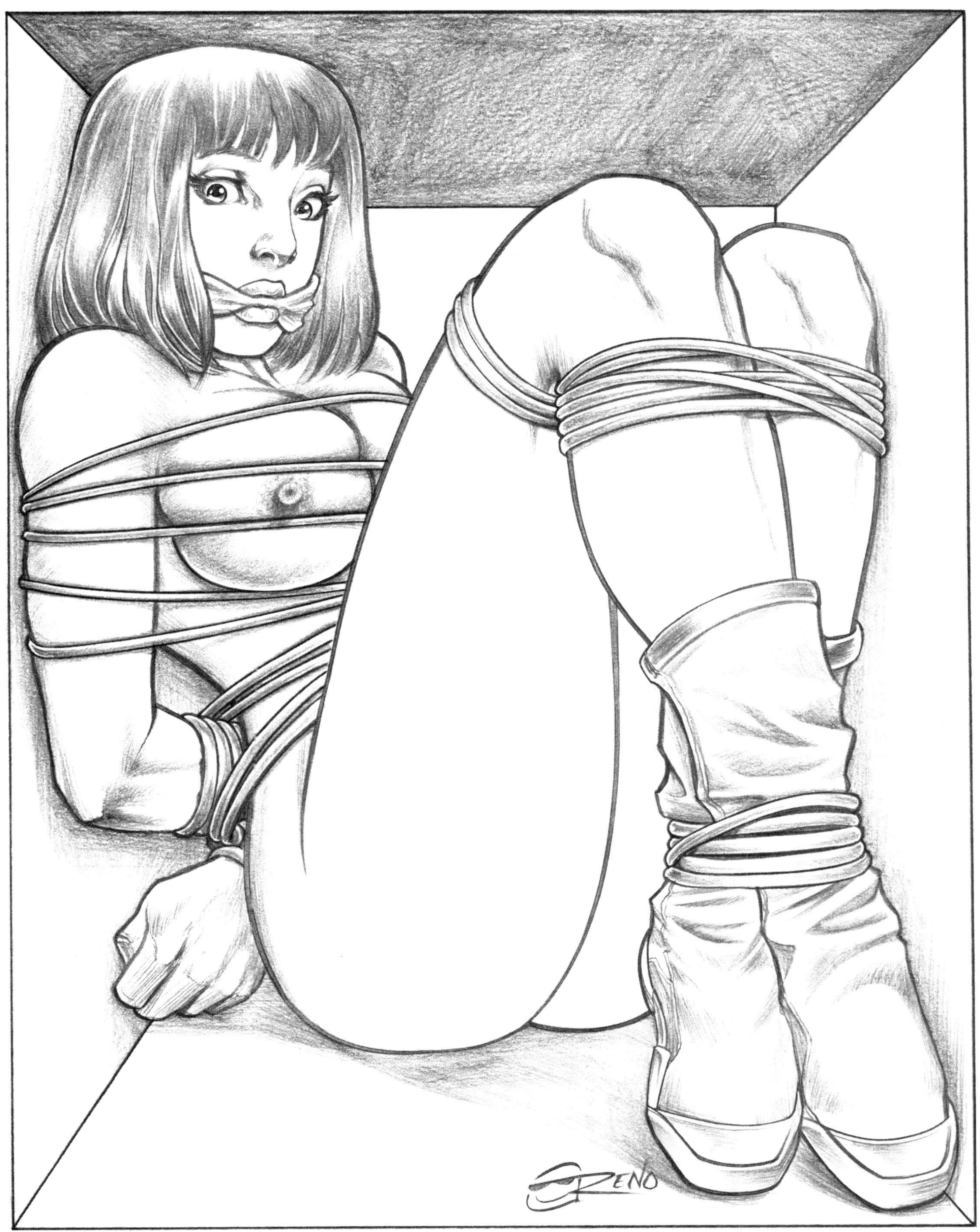


*Box Set CD2*

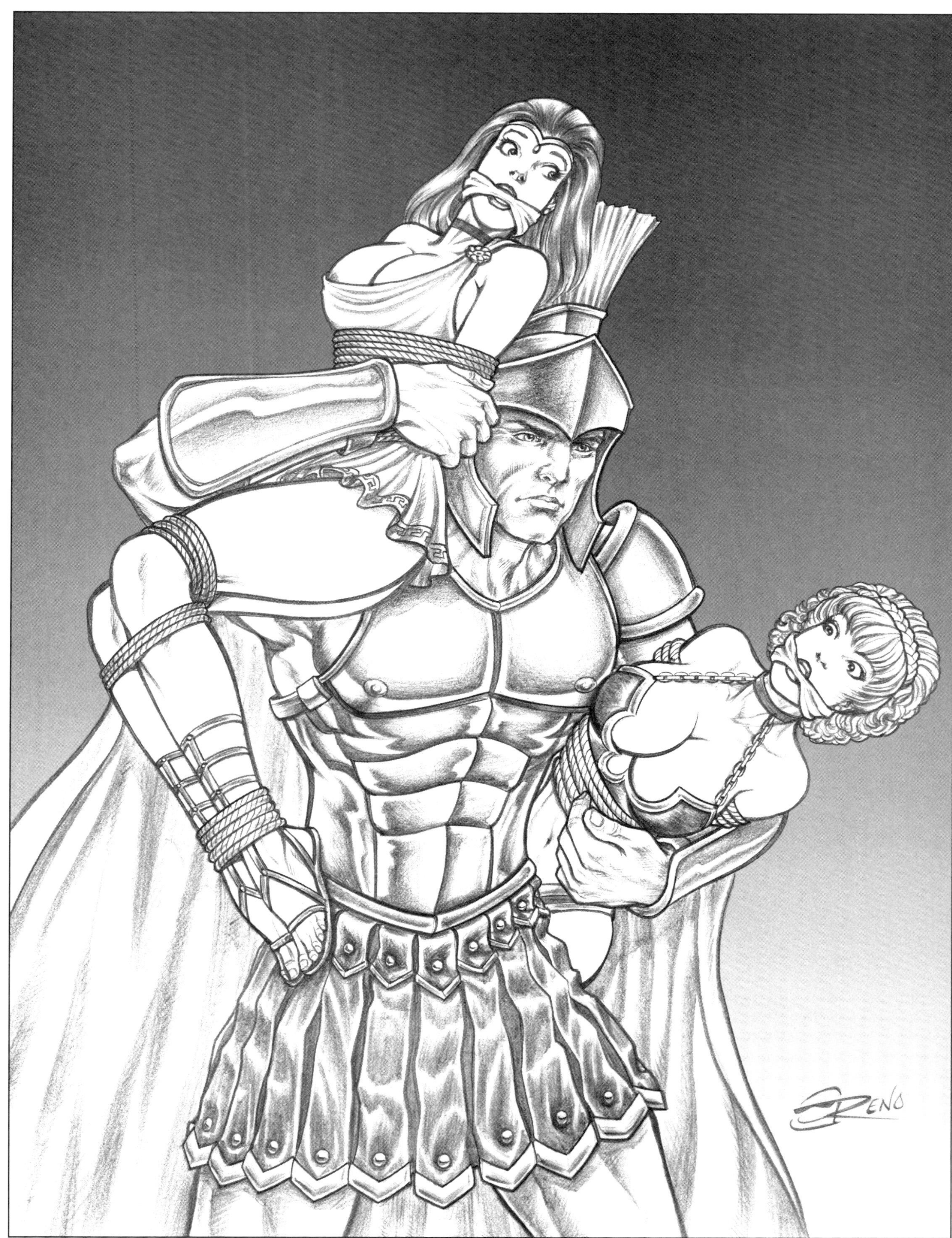


*Gladiator*

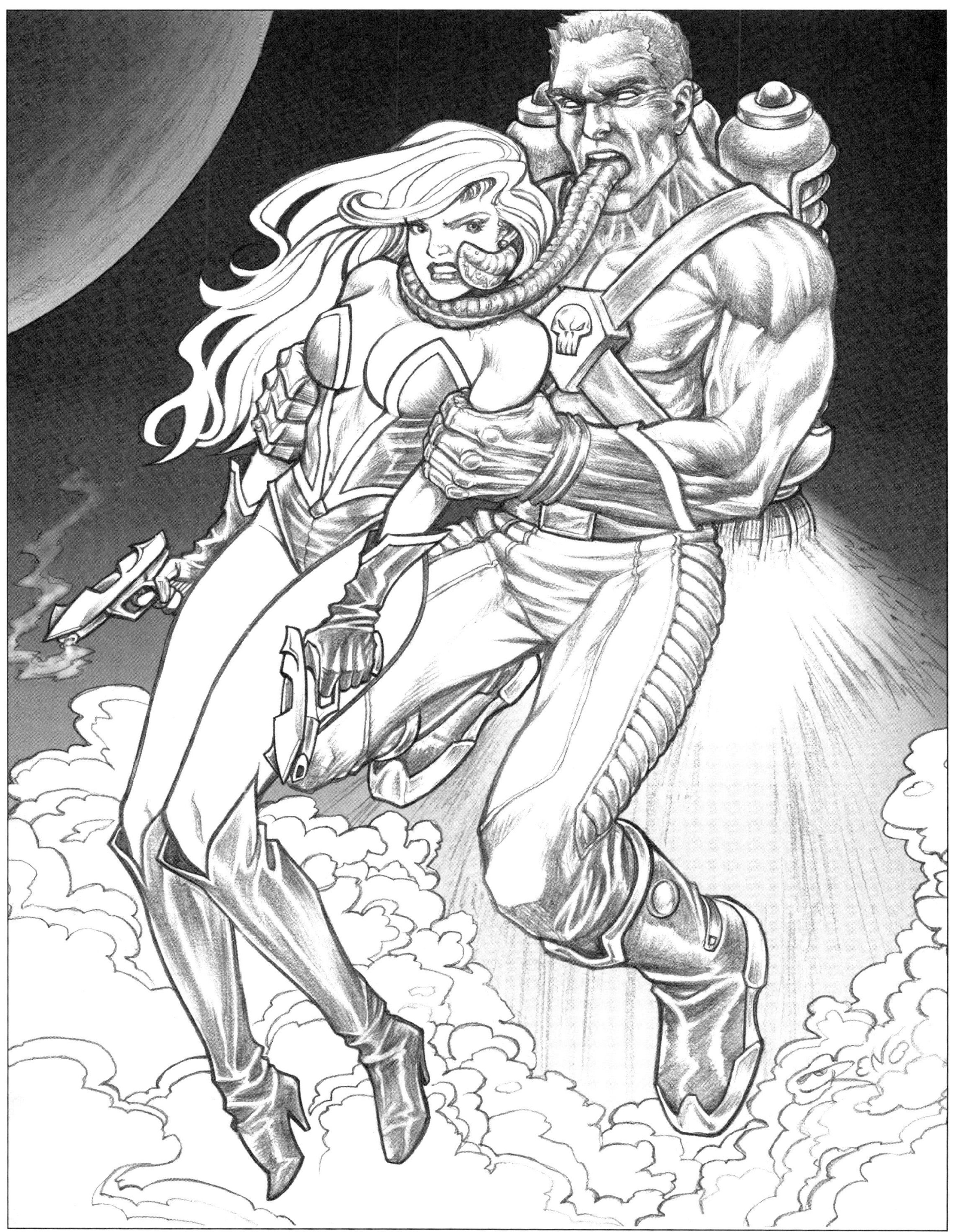

*Lust and Rockets*

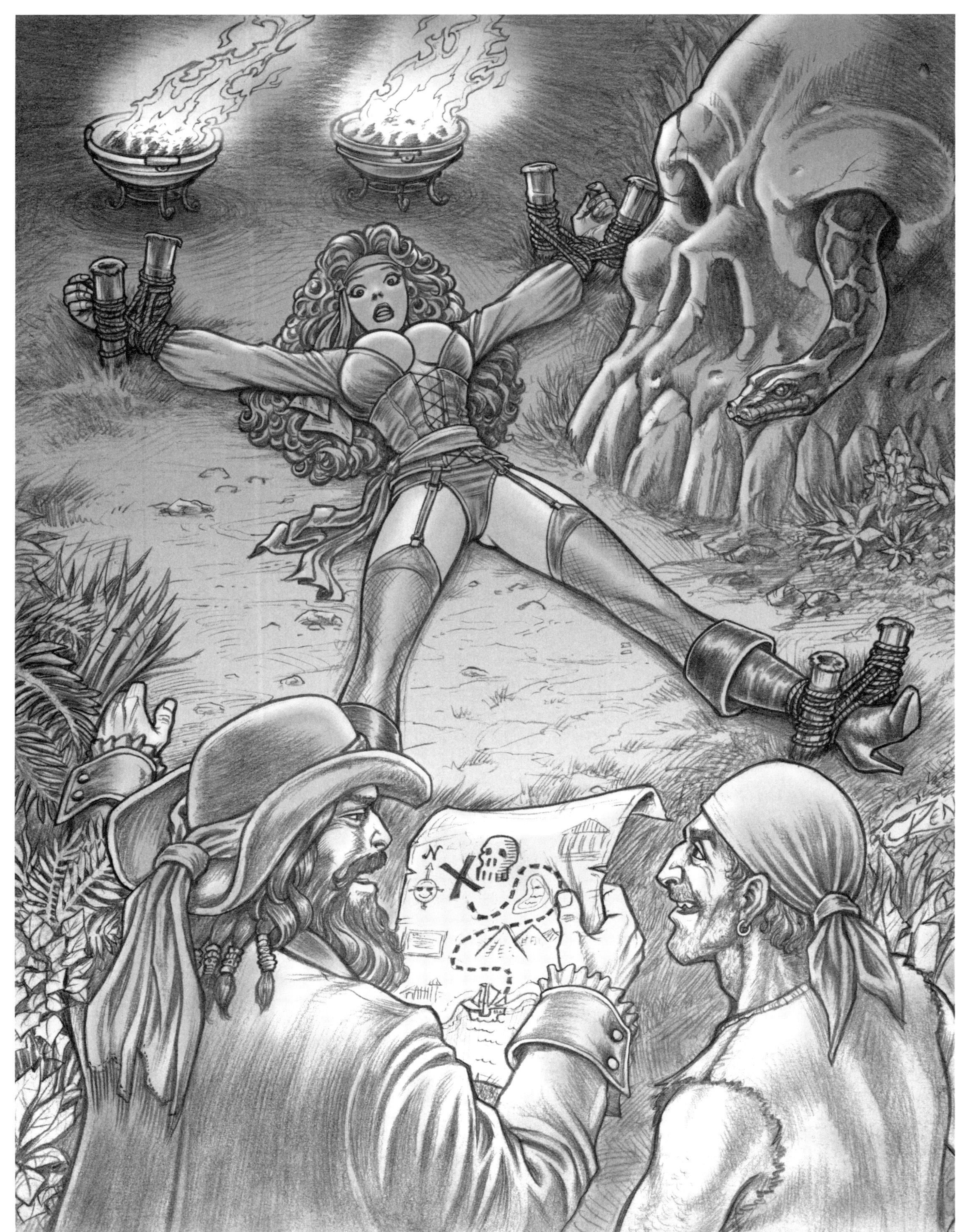


*"X" Marks the Spot*

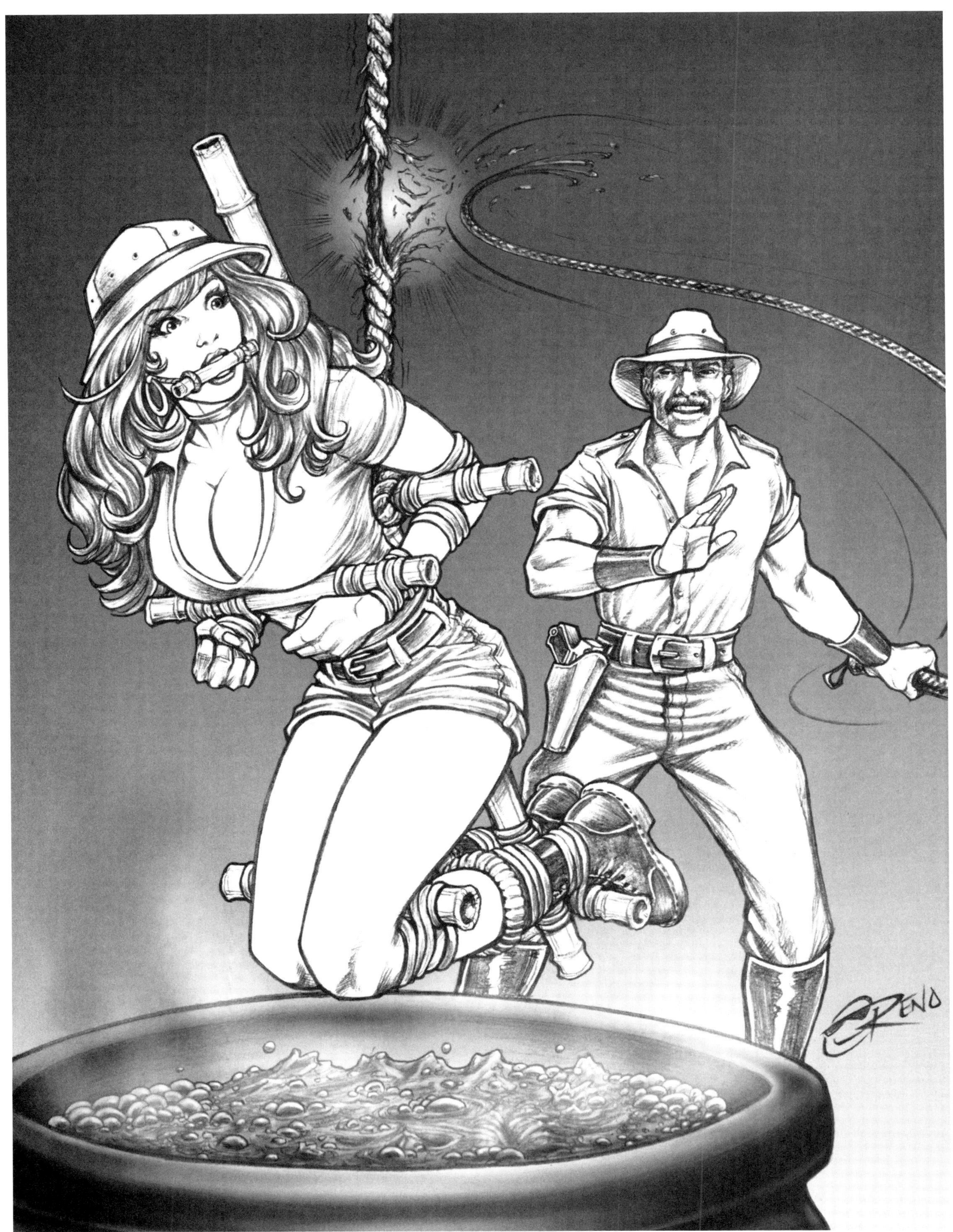


*Whipping Up Some Dinner*

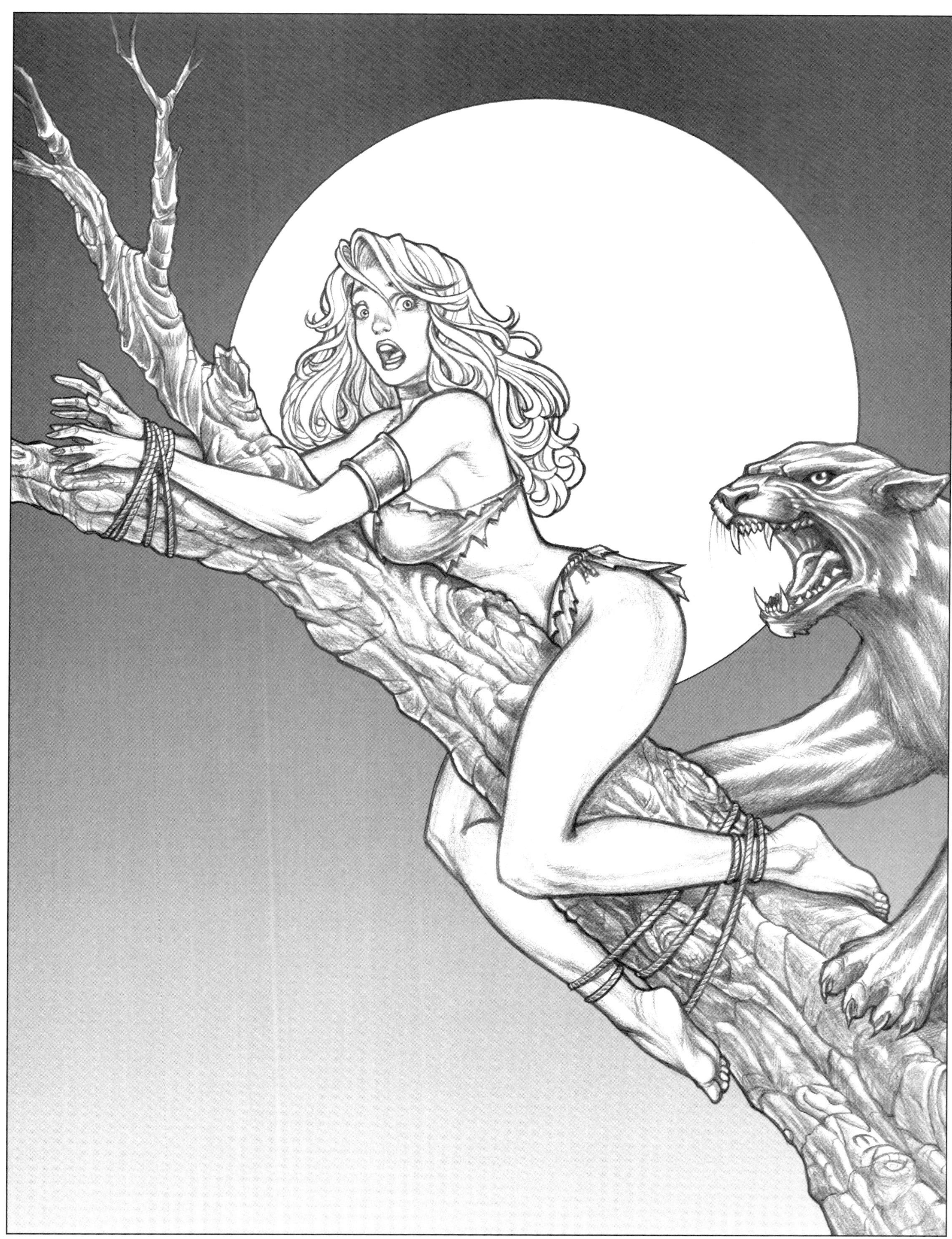

*Bad Onca*

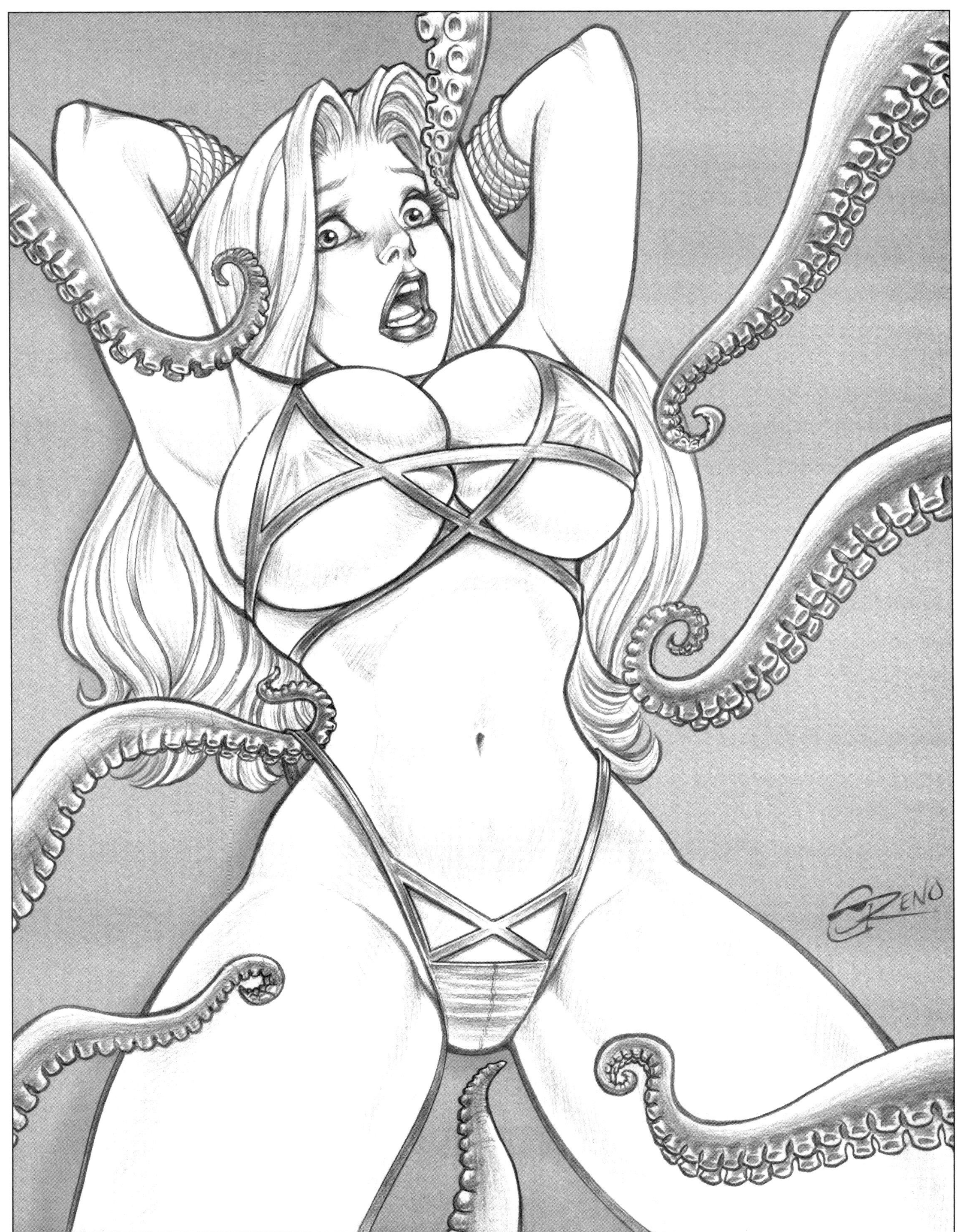

*Vulgaris*

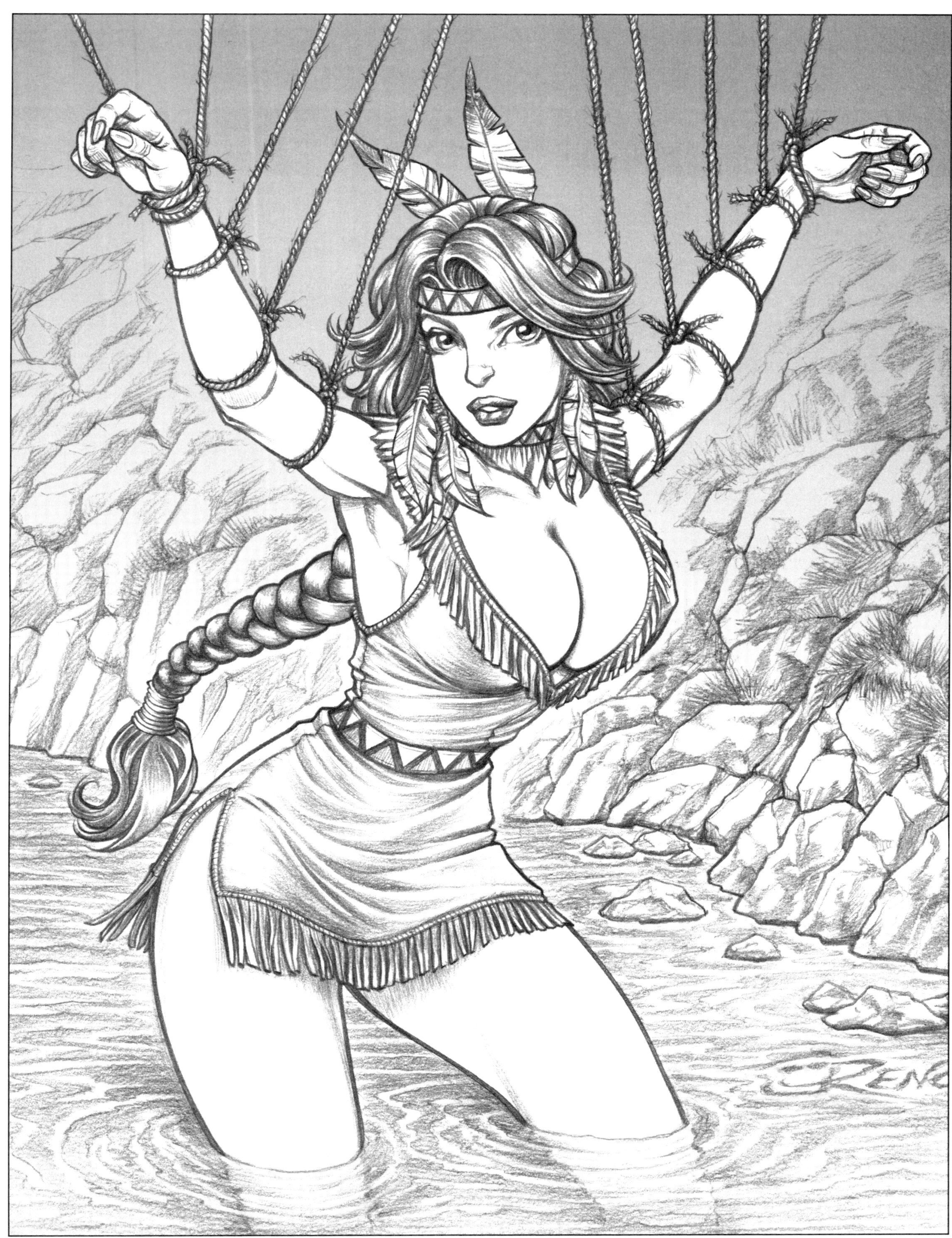

*Squaw Valley*

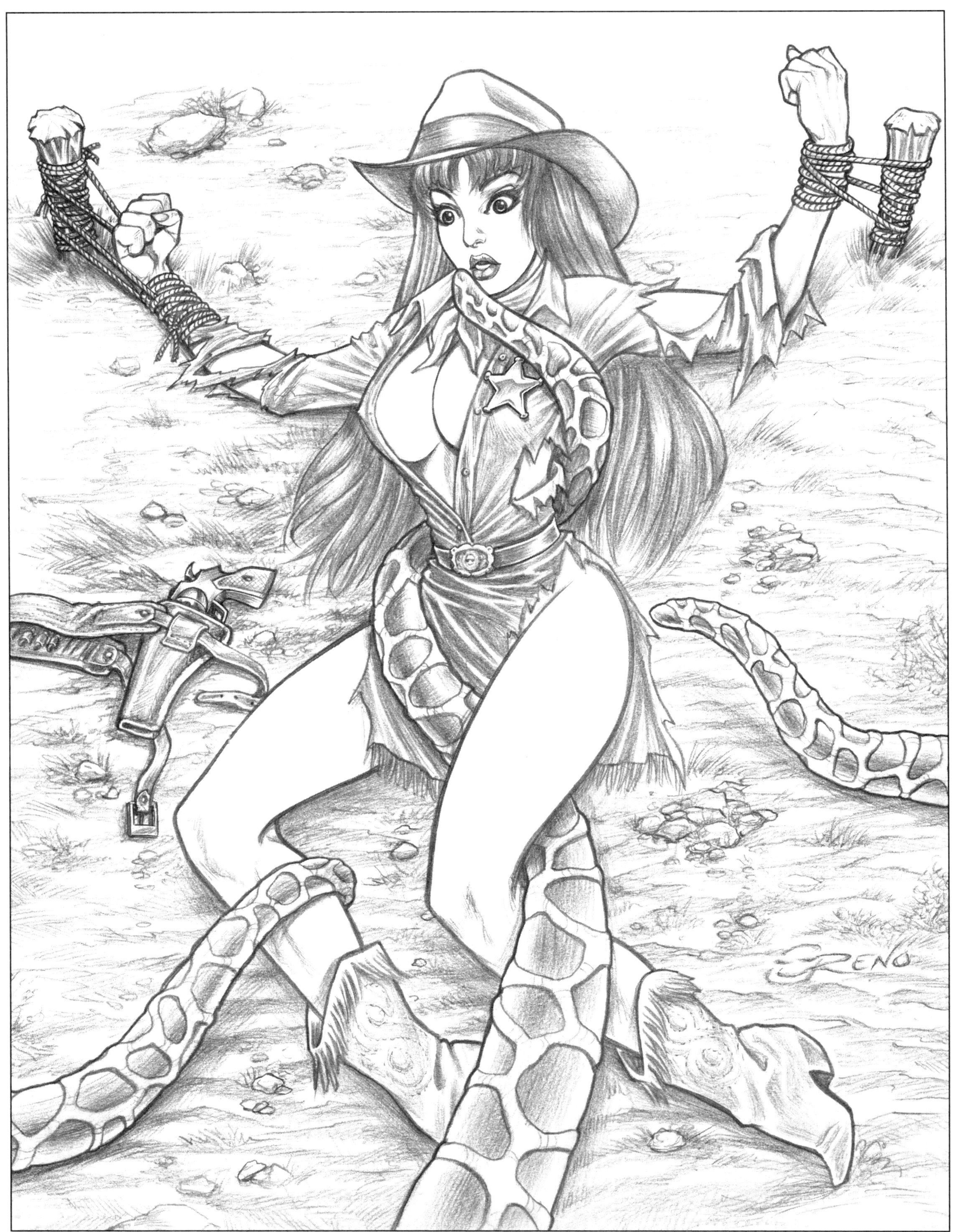


*Jailer Bait*

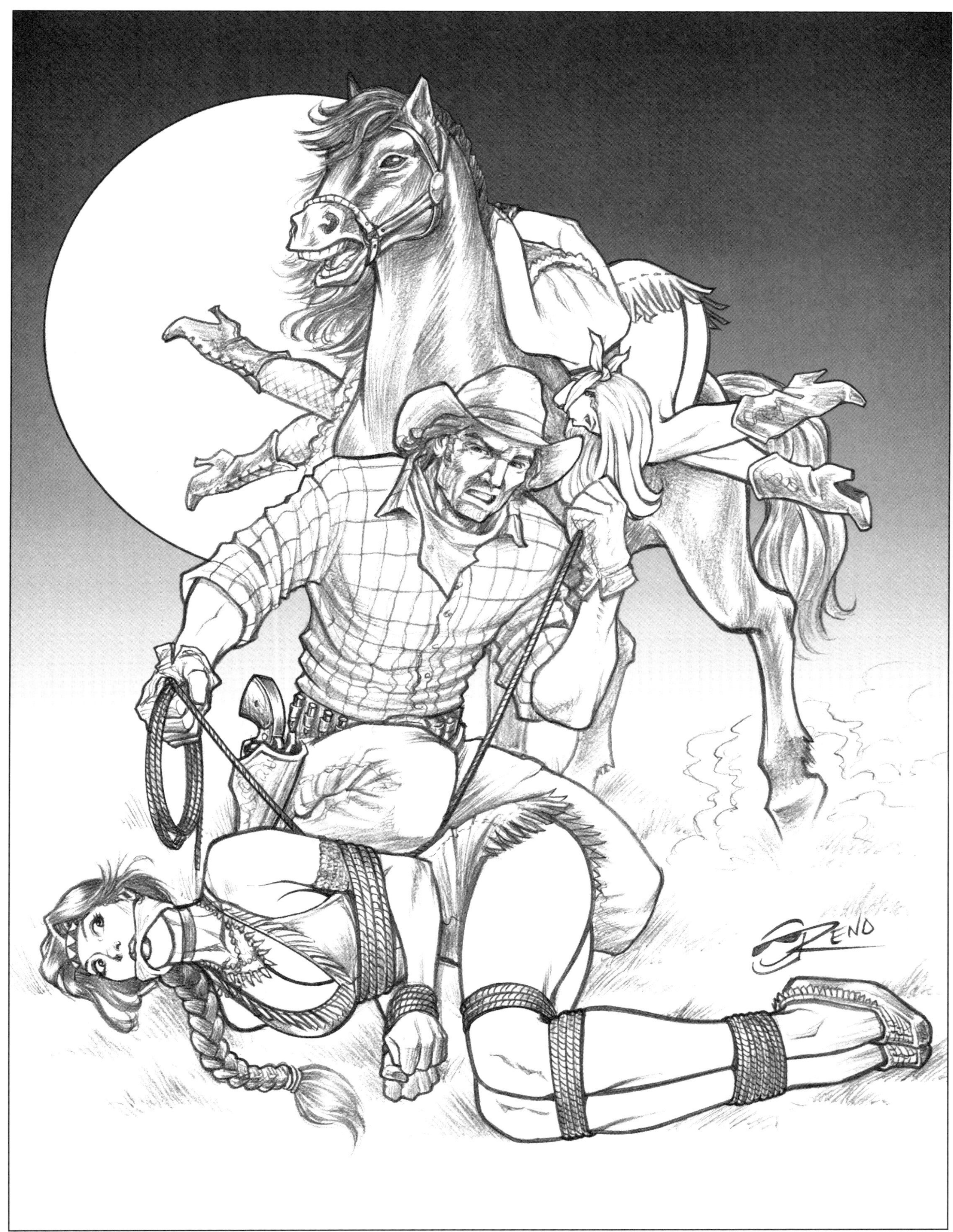

*Round Up*

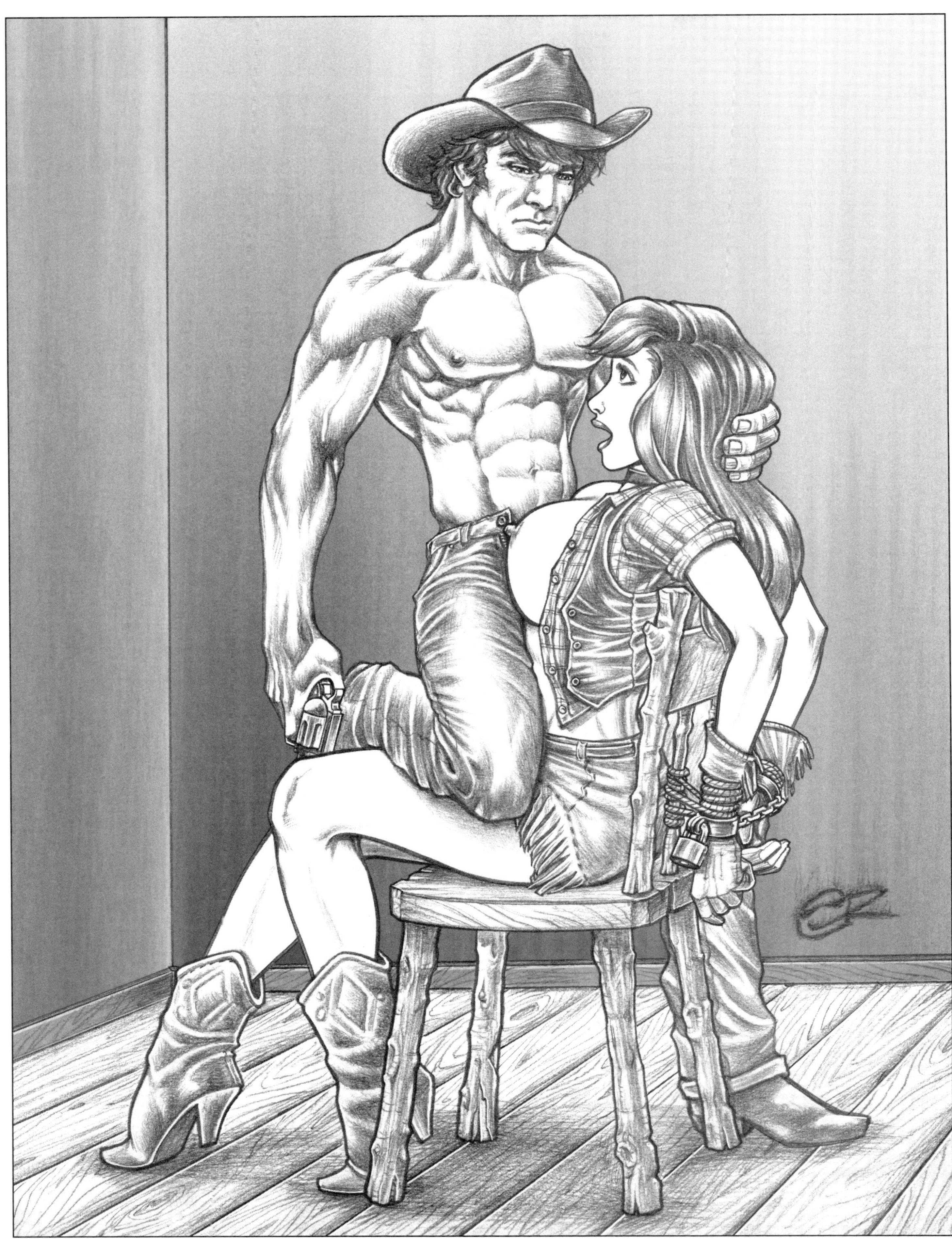

*Mount Up*

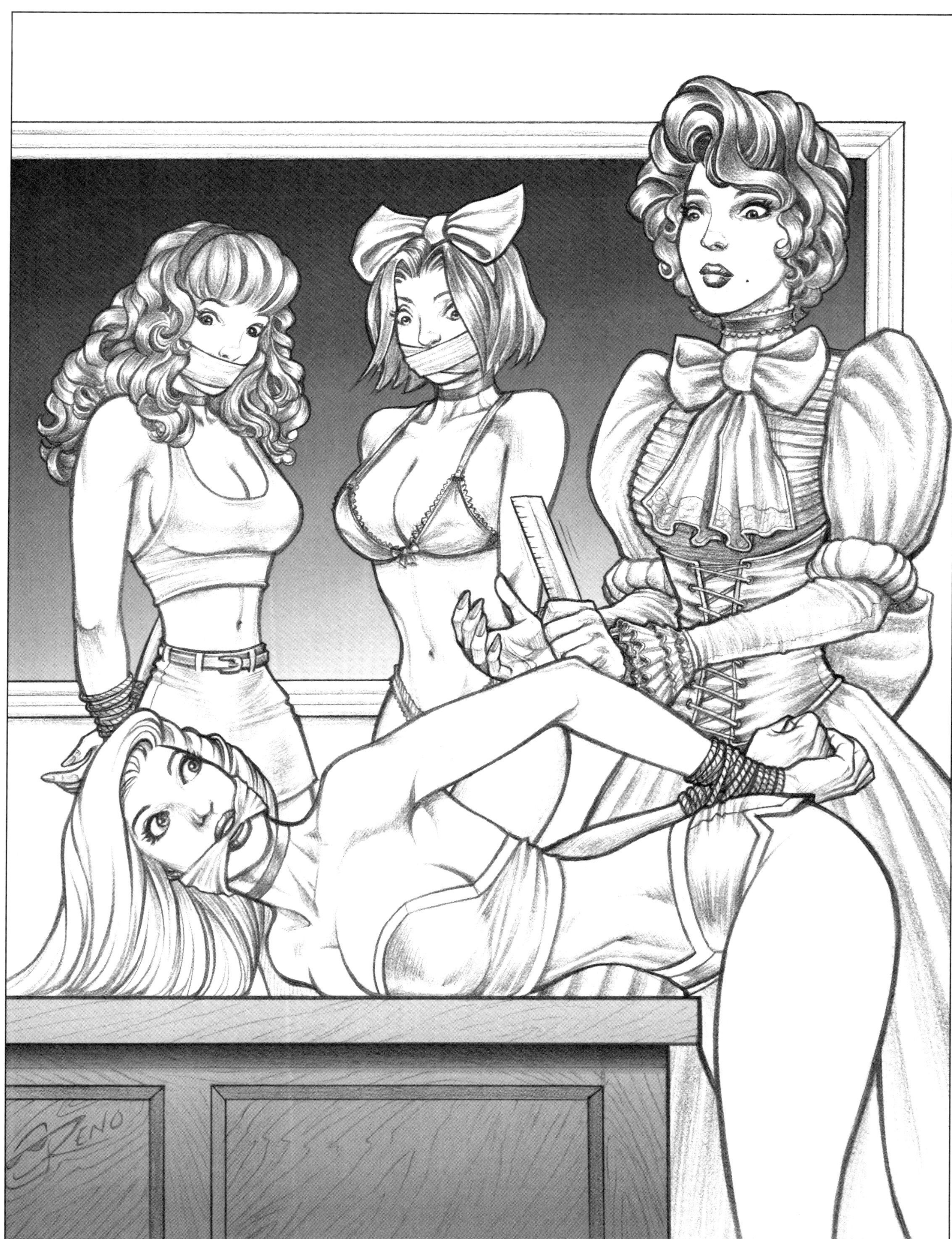

*Old Fashioned Lesson*

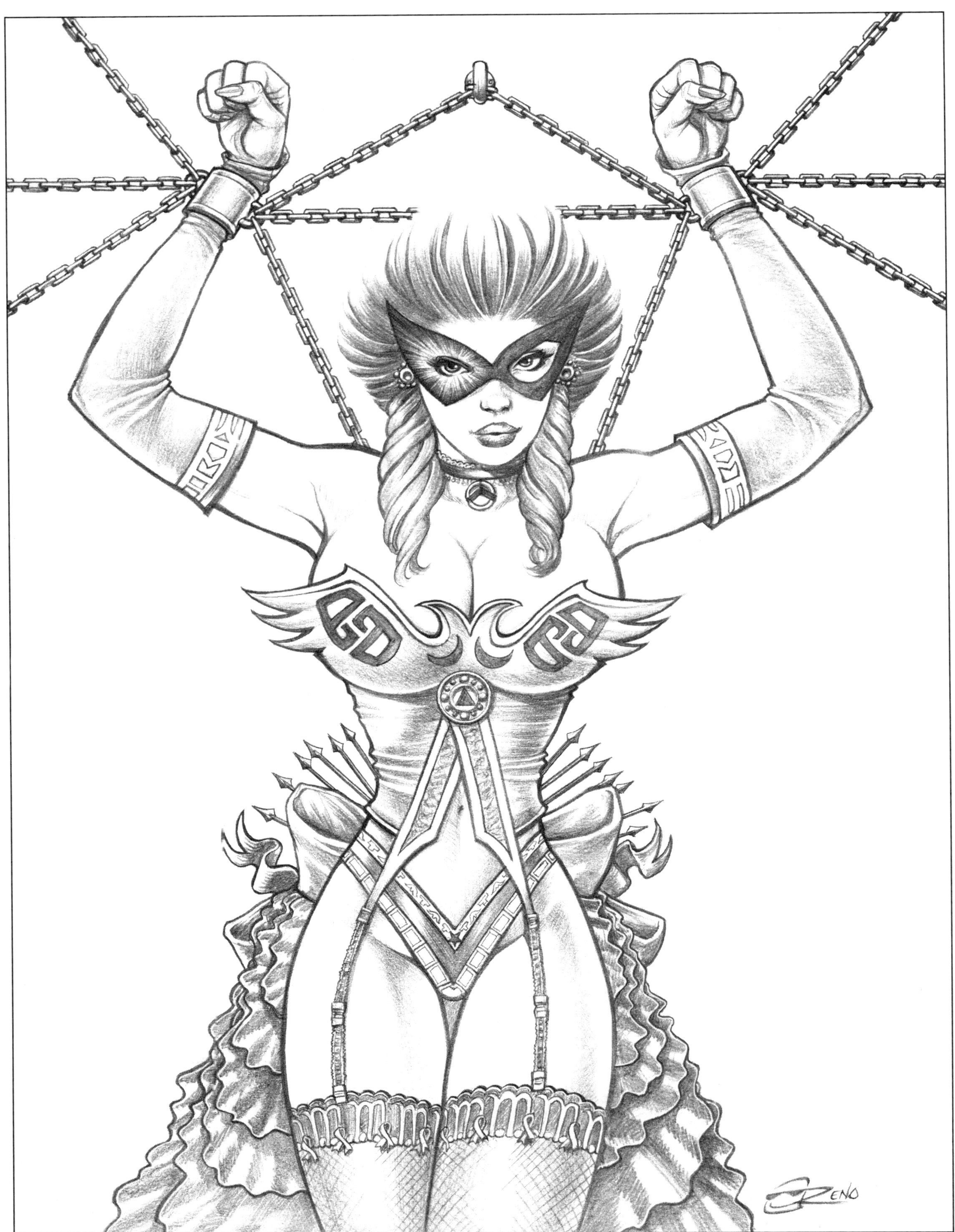


*IllumiNaughty*

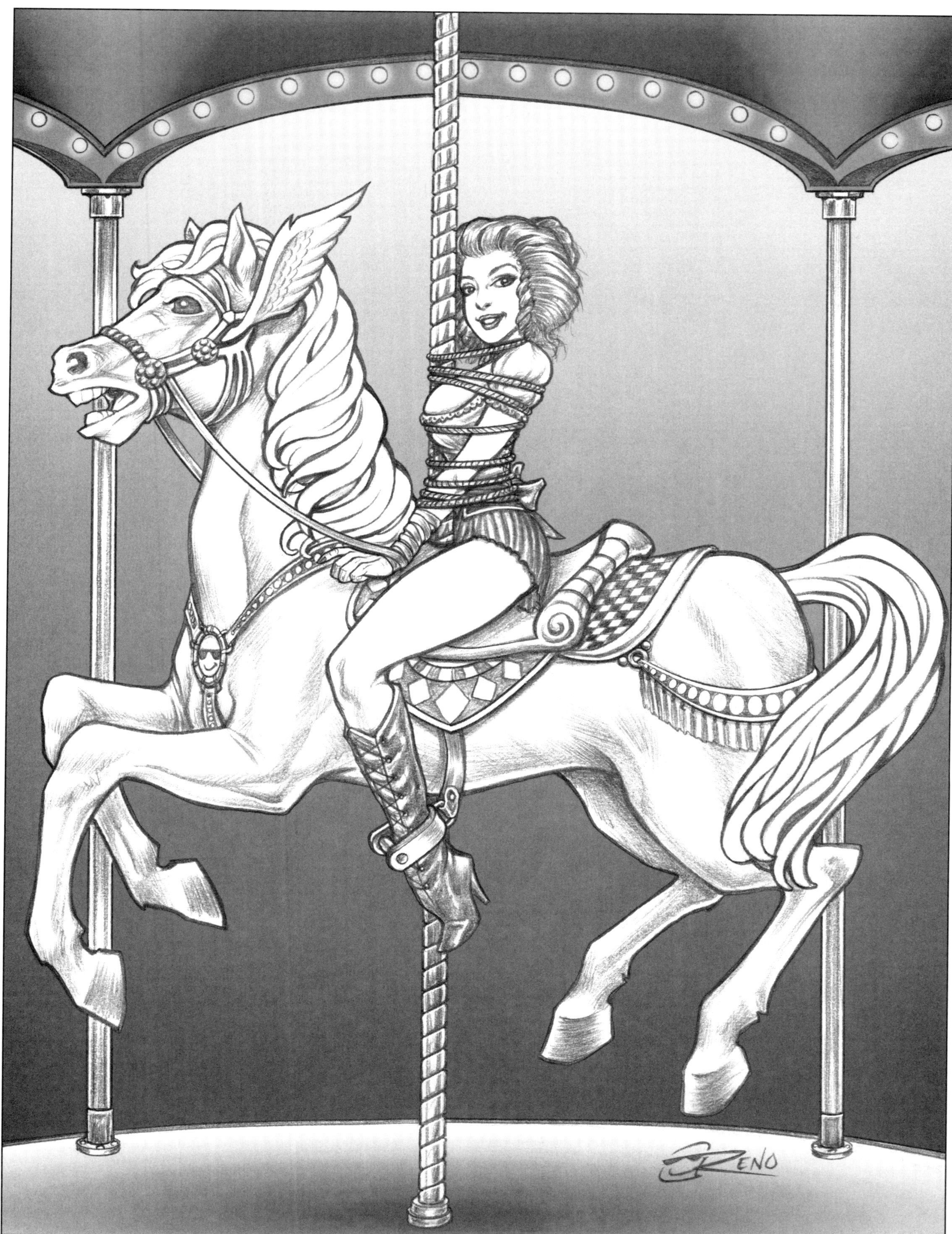

*Mary Got Bound*

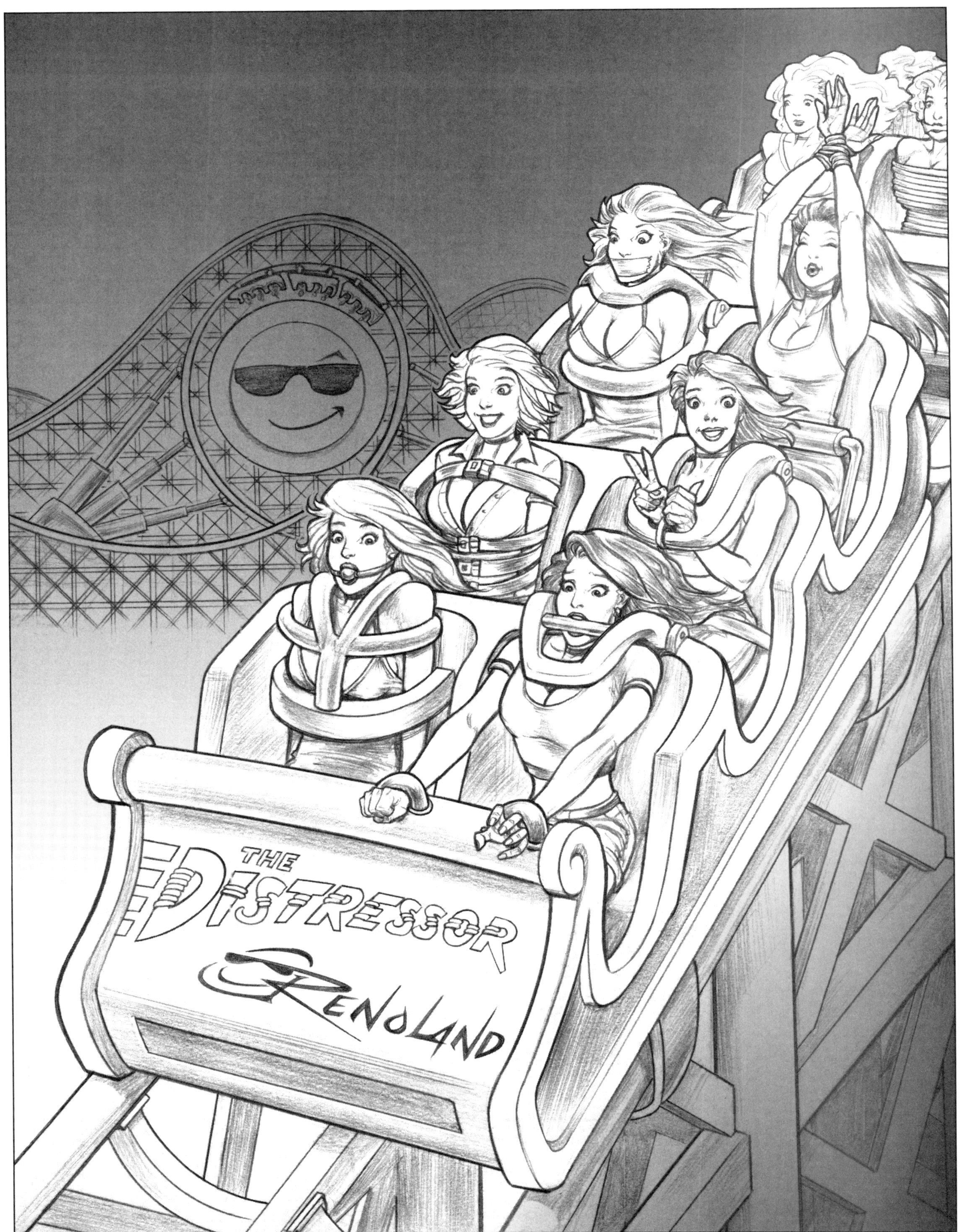


*The Distressor*

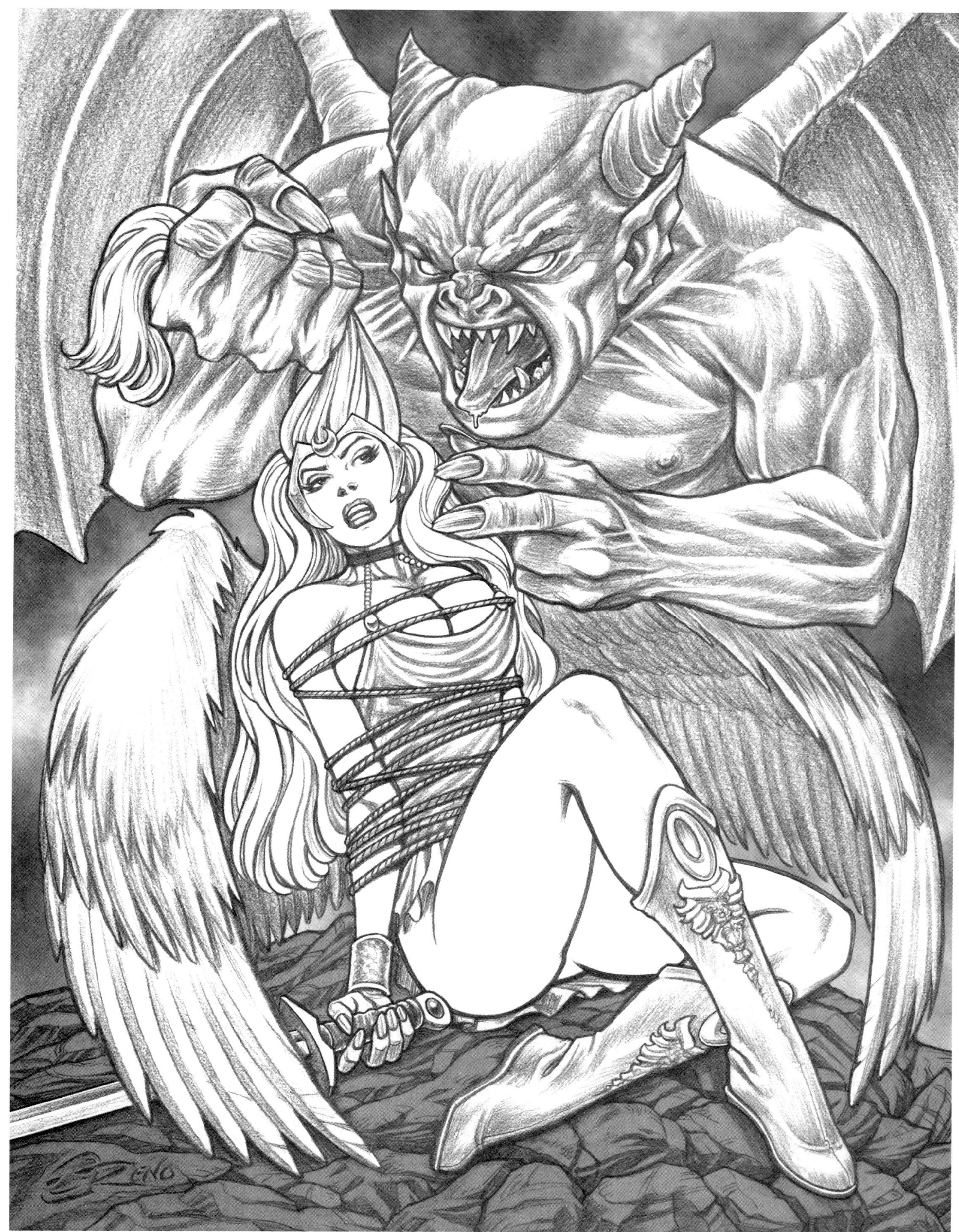


*Fallen Angel*

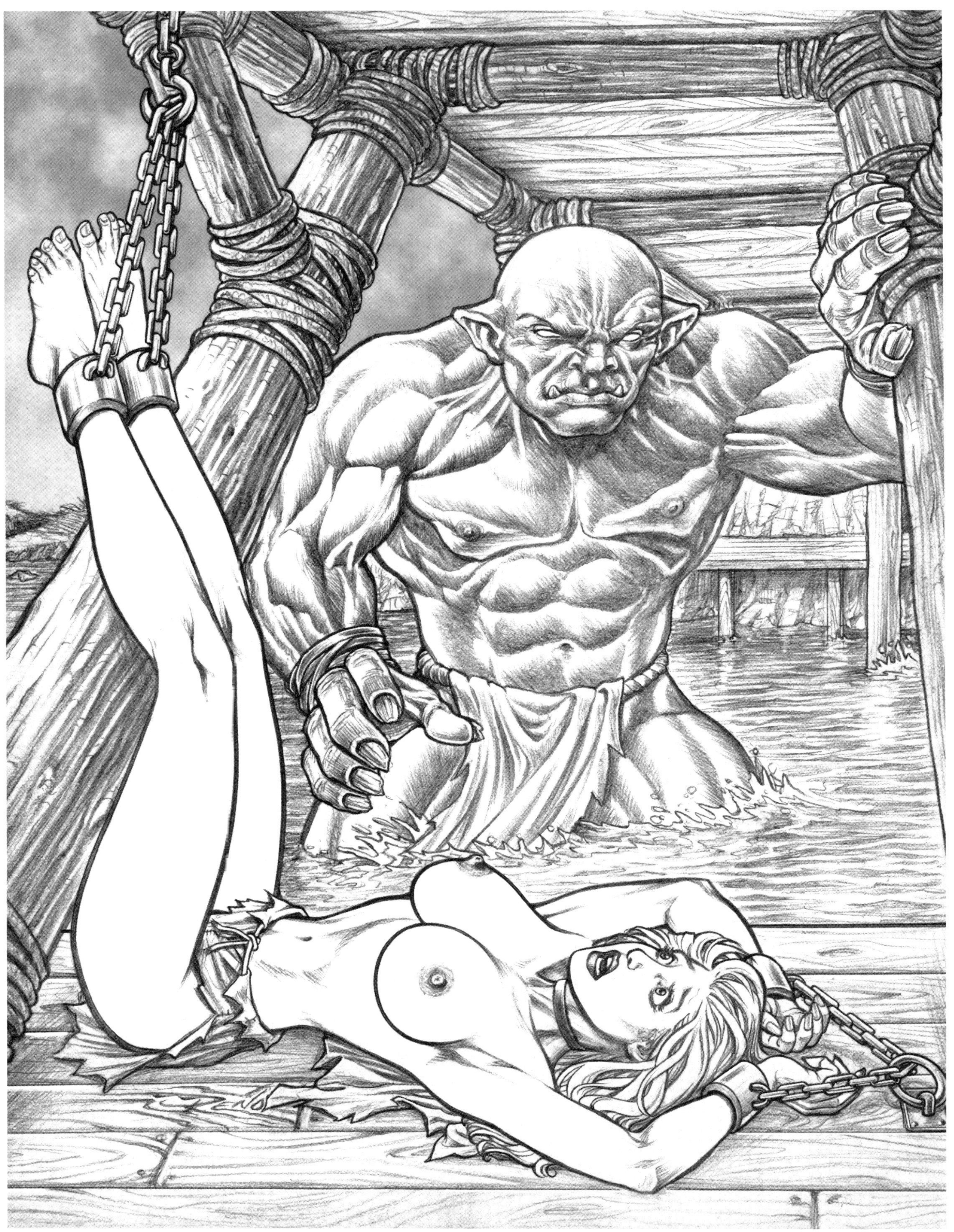

*Trolling For Trolls*

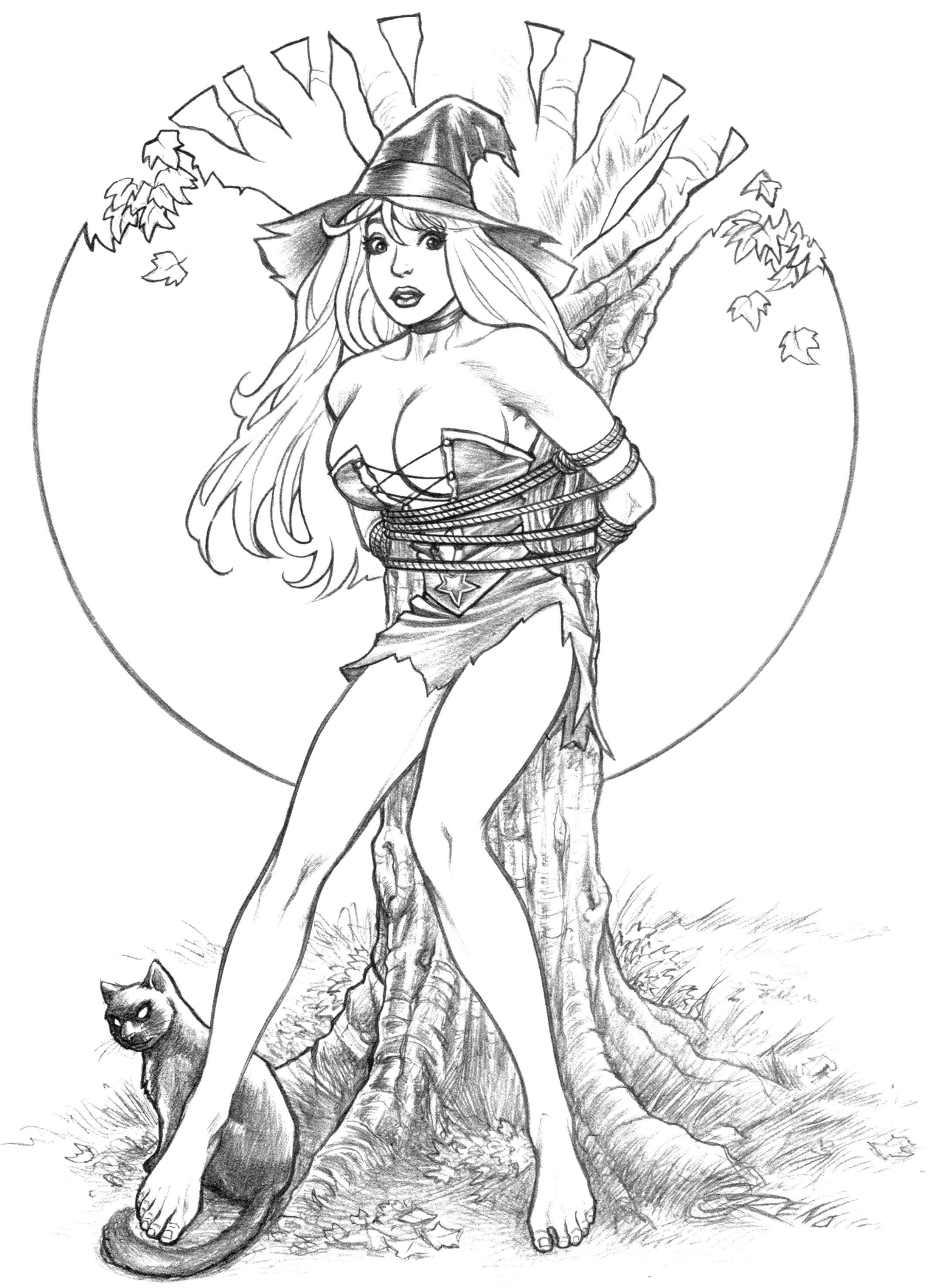

*Tricked Treat*

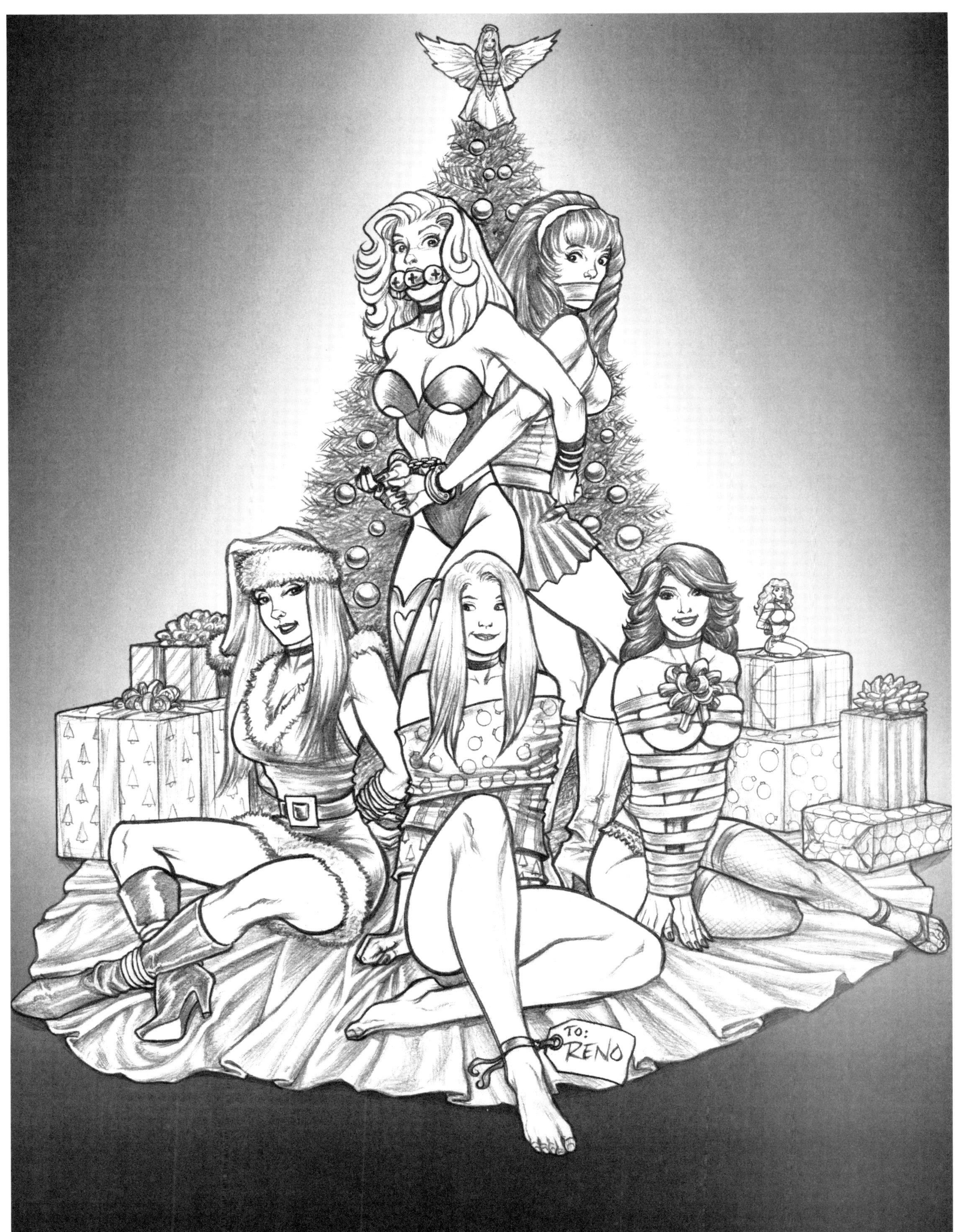


*All I Want For Christmas*

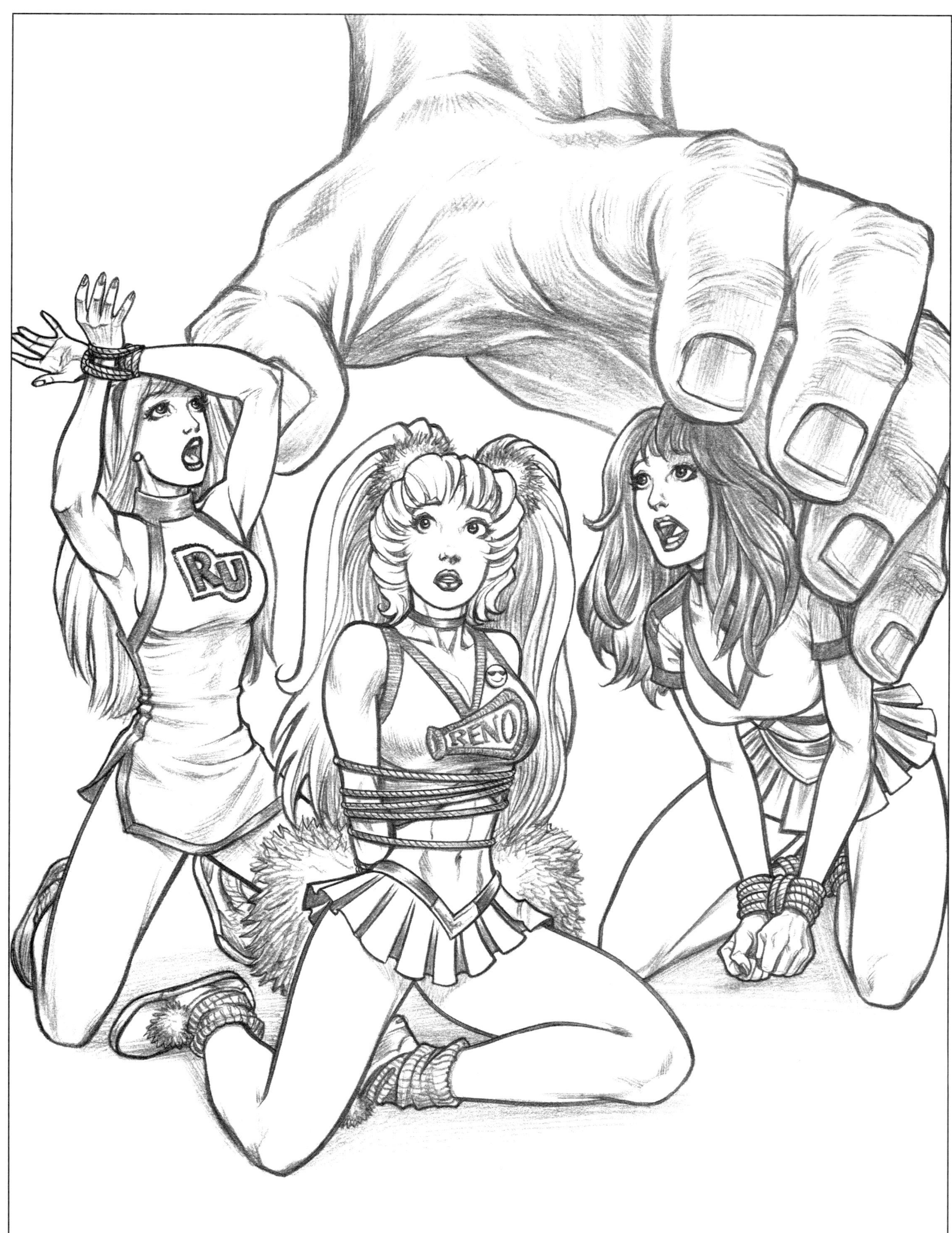


*Good Cheer*

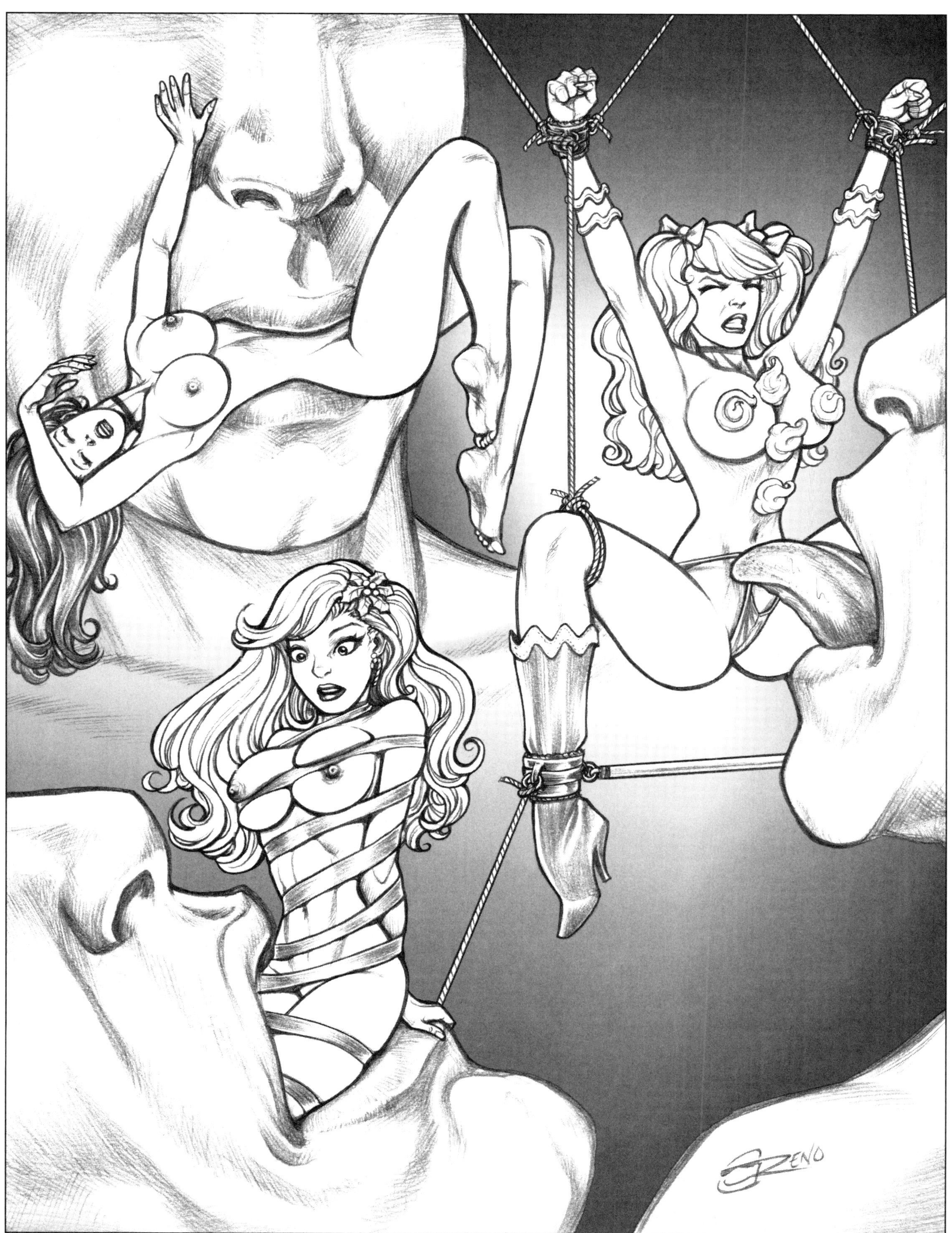

*Holiday Treats*

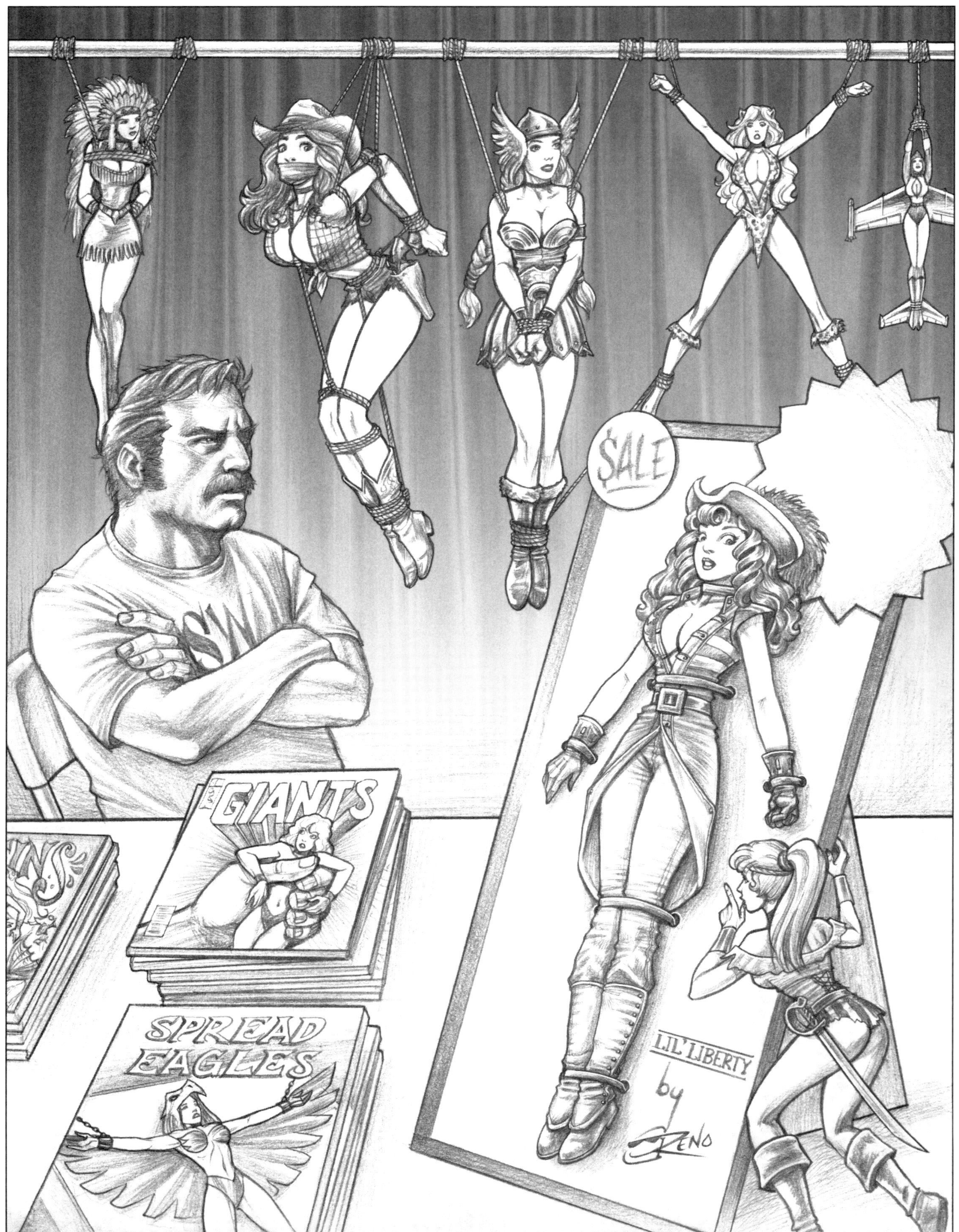


SWFL

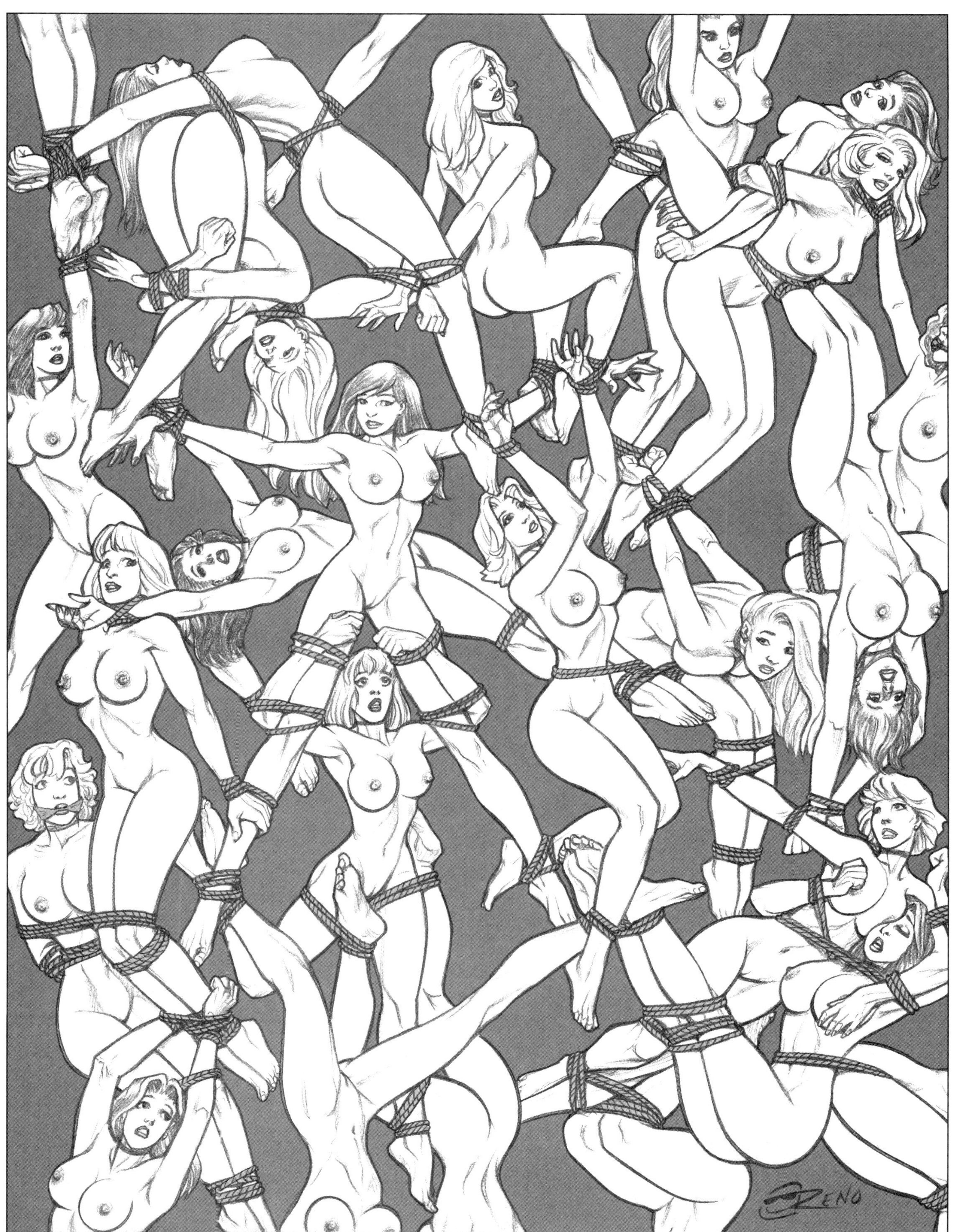

*Wall Of Fame*

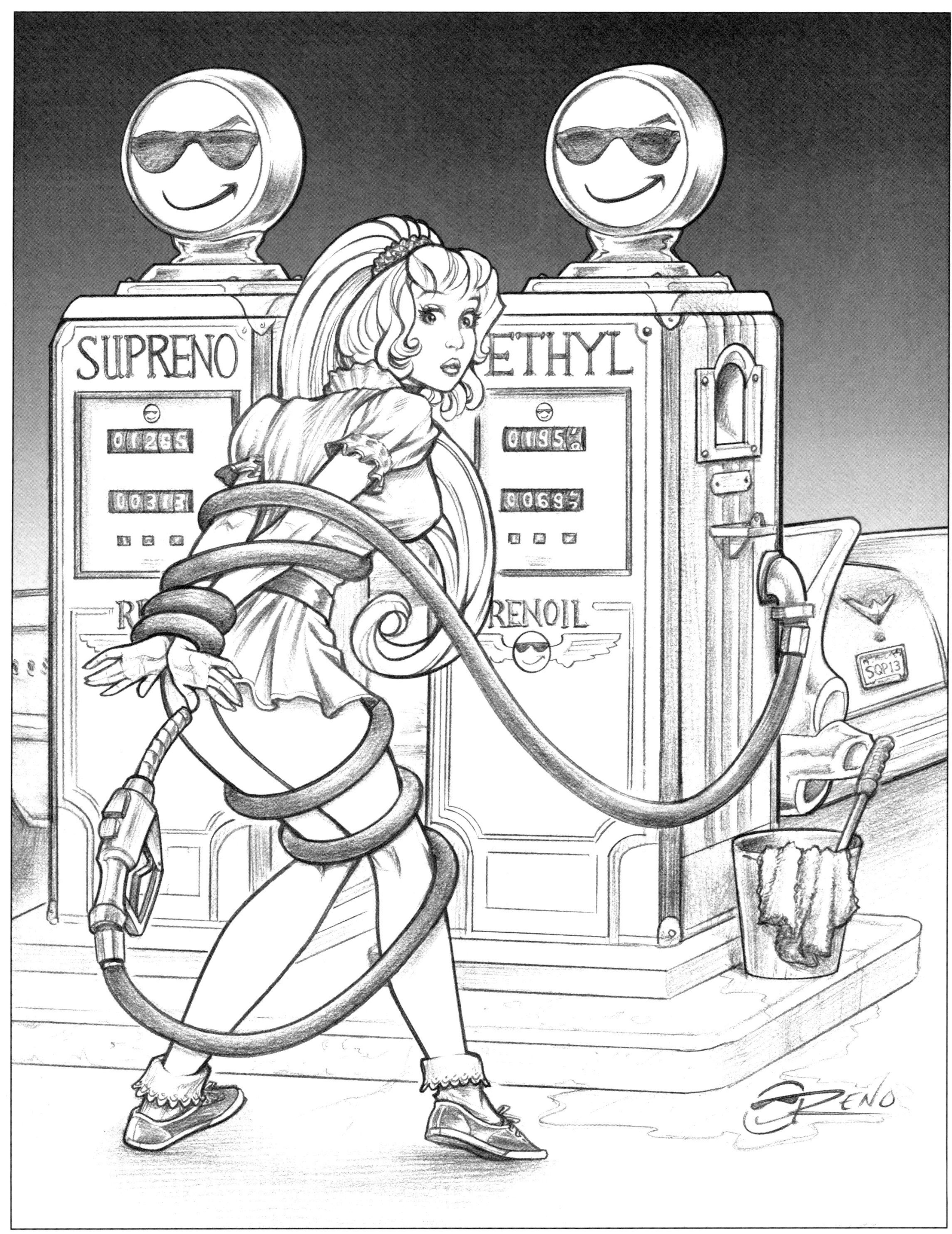


*Pumping Ethyl*

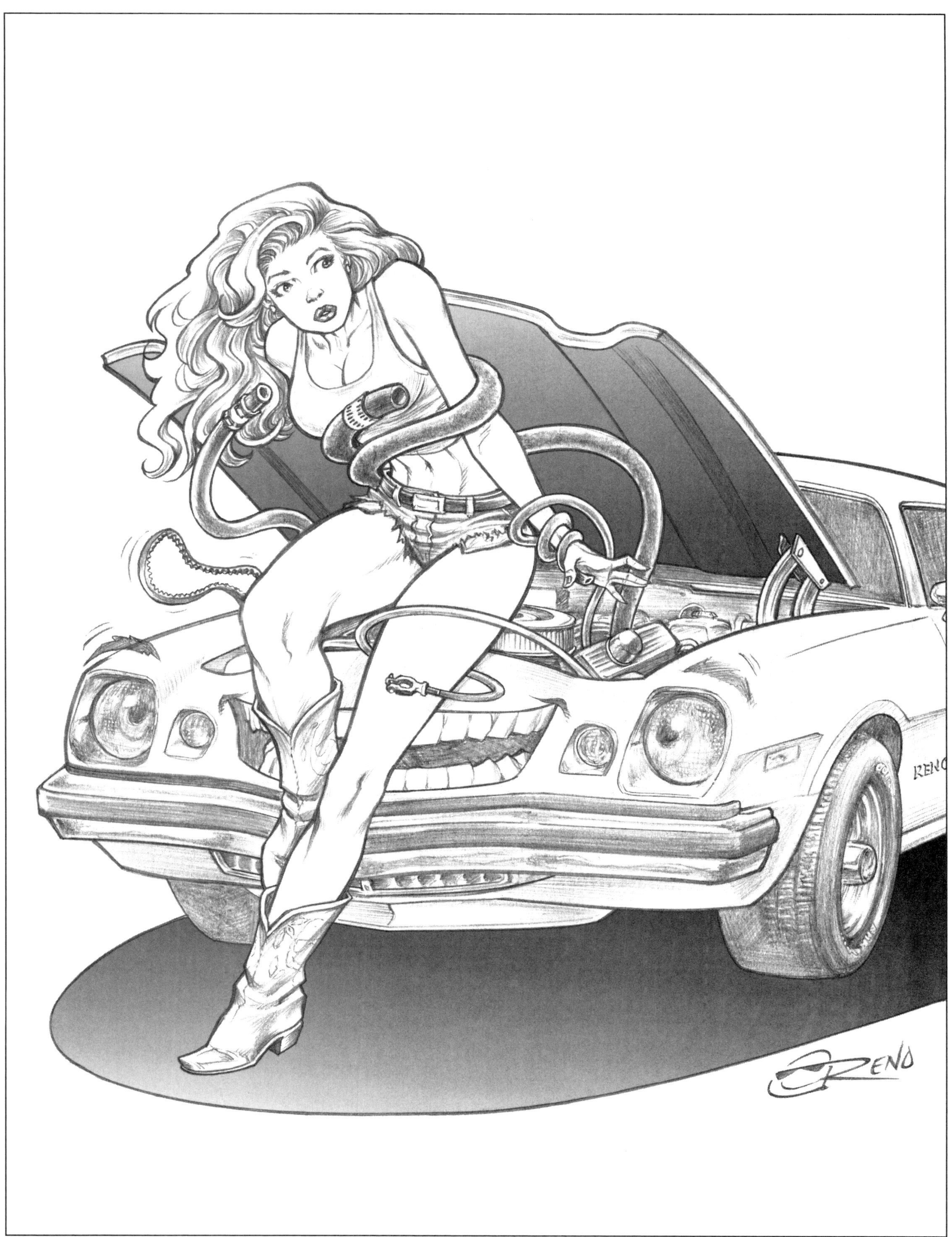


*CARpe Dame*

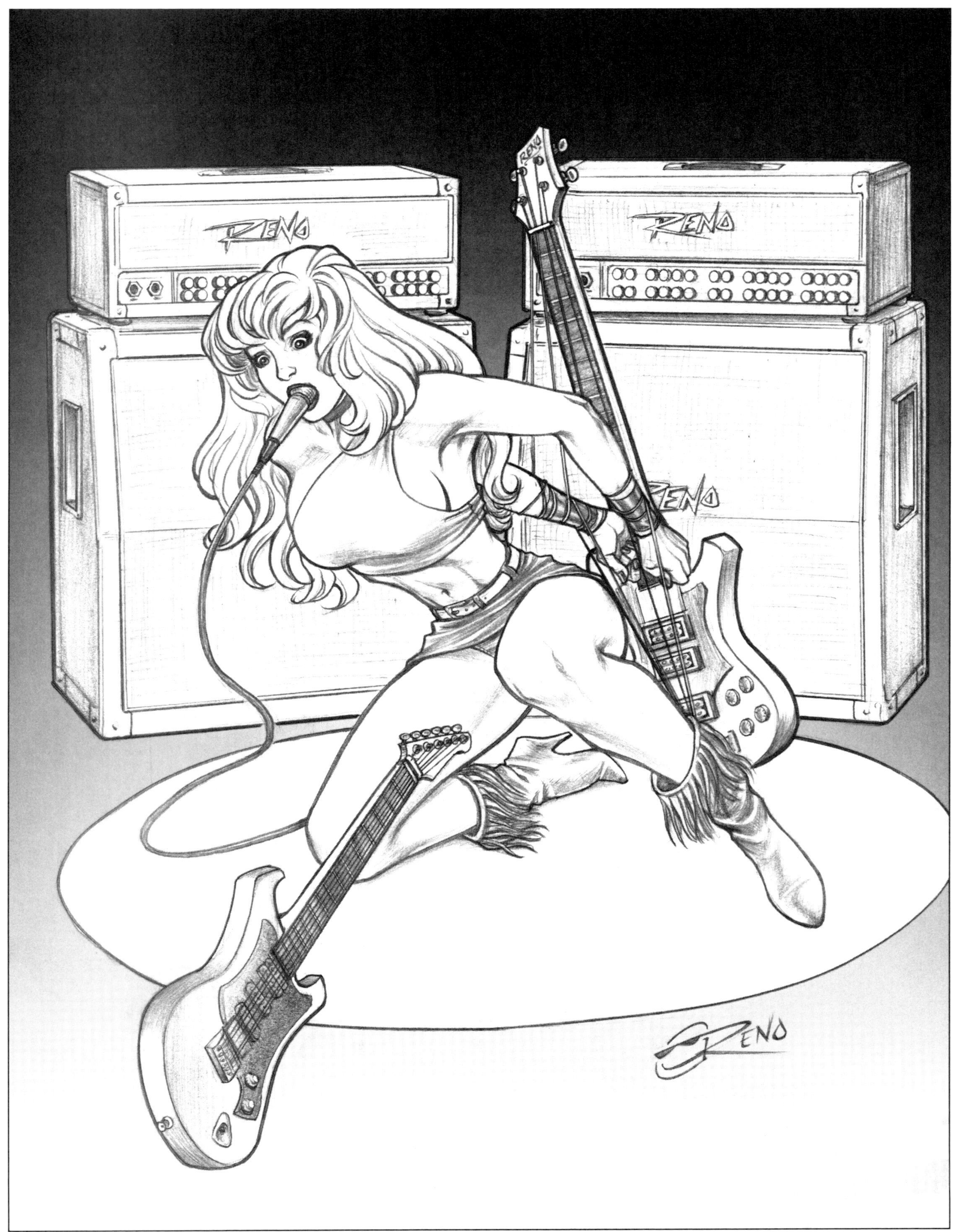


*Rock Your Body*

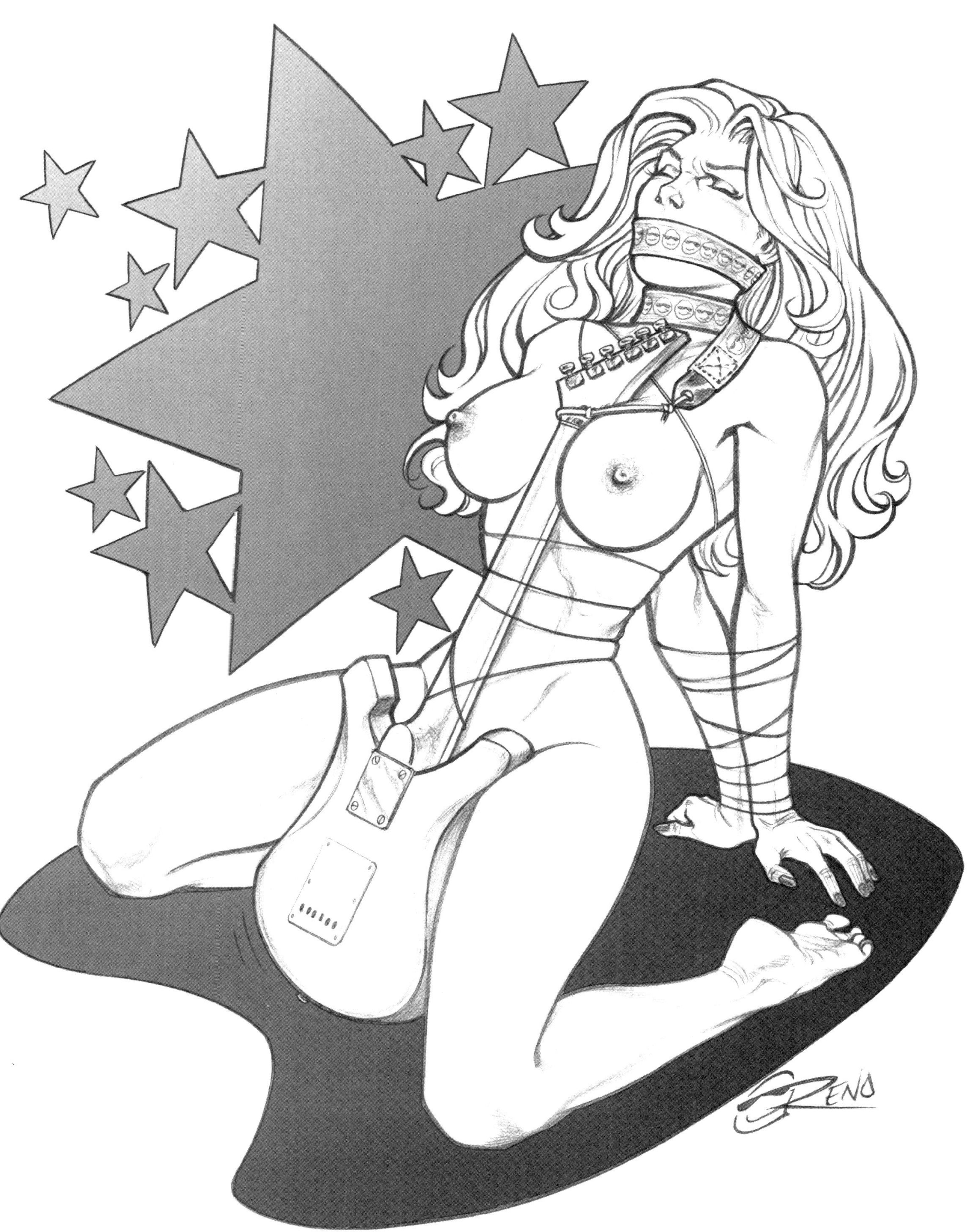

*GuitSome*

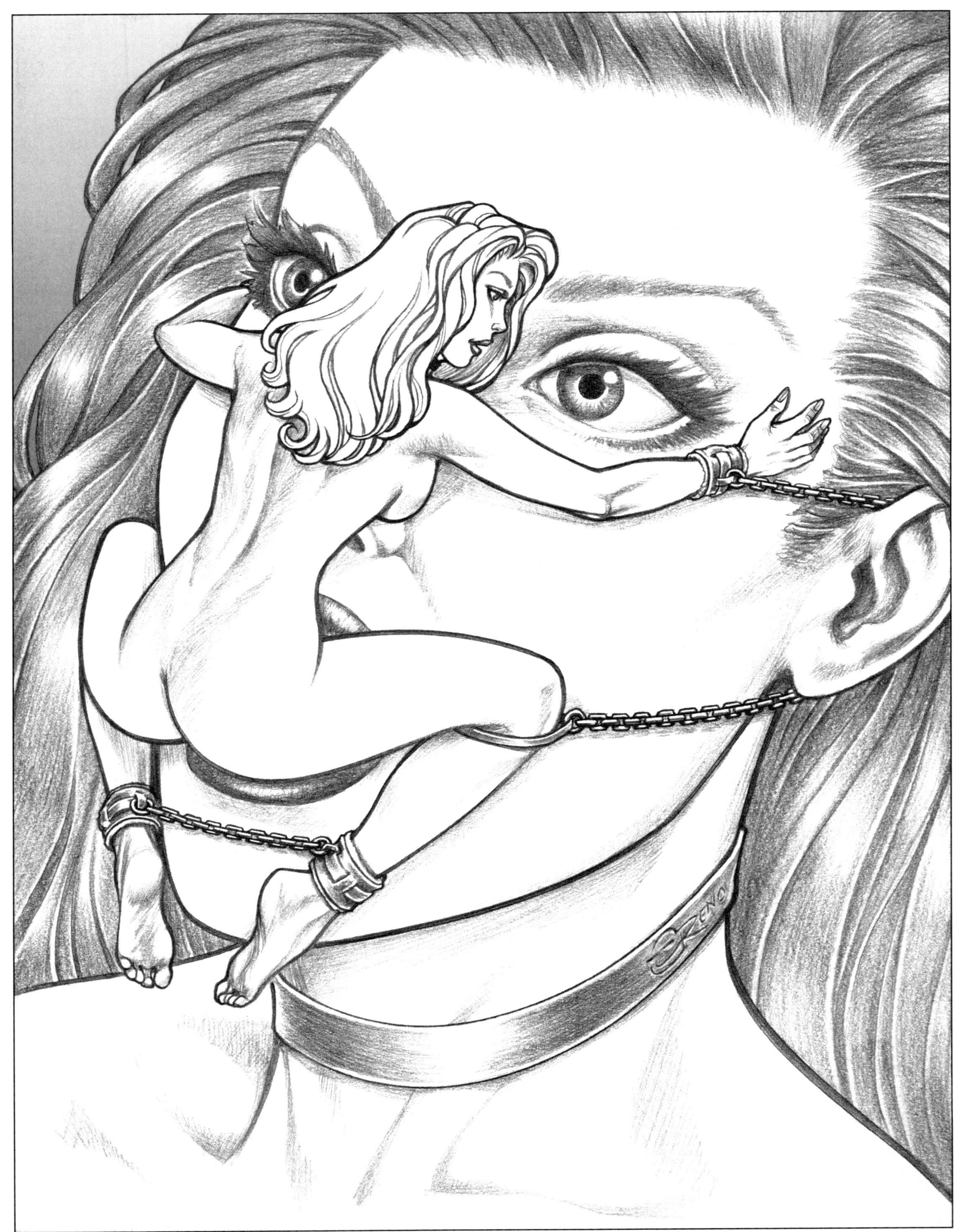

*A Bound Face*

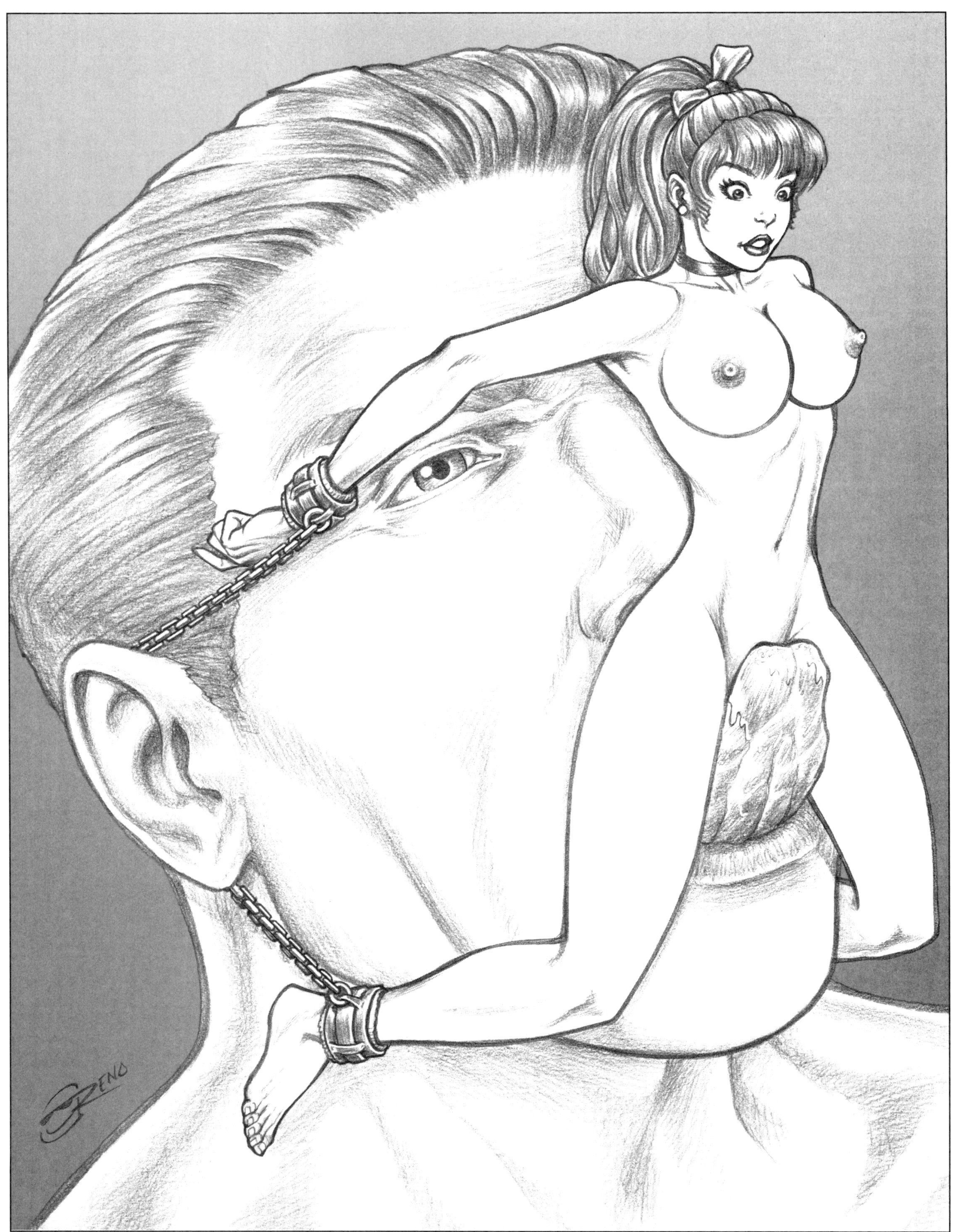

*Tip of the Tongue*

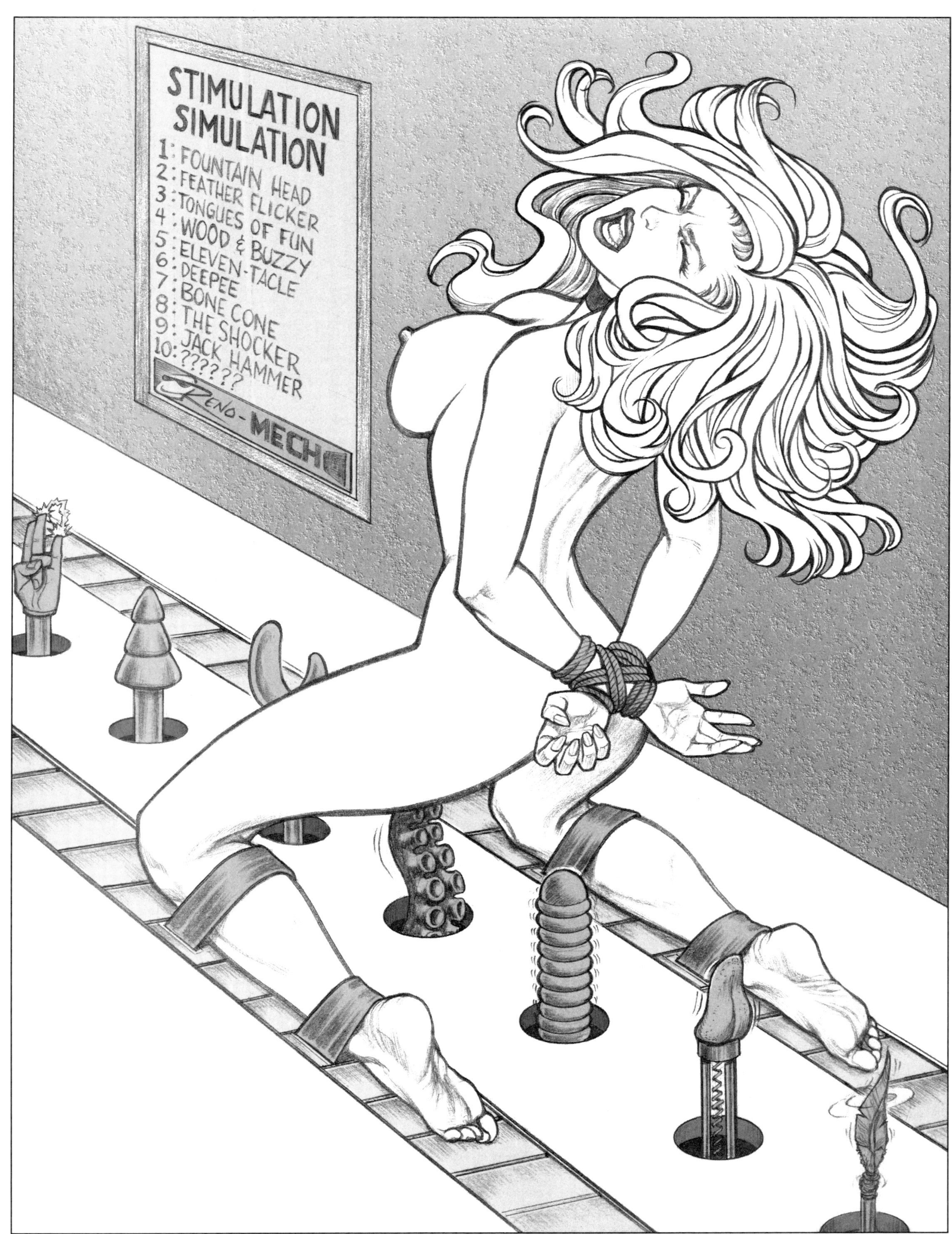


*The Gauntlet*